Microsoft® .NET™

Jumpstart for Systems Administrators and Developers

Microsoft® .NET™
Jumpstart for Systems Administrators and Developers

Nigel Stanley

Digital Press
An imprint of Elsevier Science
Amsterdam • Boston • London • New York • Oxford • Paris • San Diego
San Francisco • Singapore • Sydney • Tokyo

Library of Congress Cataloging-in-Publication Data
Nigel, Stanley
    .NET : jump start for administrators, and power users / Stanley Nigel.
       p. cm.
    ISBN: 1-55558-285-0
    1. Microsoft .NET, I. Title

QA76.76.M52N542003
005.2'768–dc21

                                        2002041272

British Library Cataloguing-in-Publication Data
A catalogue record for this book is available from the British Library.

To Rue, for being there, again.

Contents

Preface

This book has come about following desperate attempts by the author to understand what .NET really means to information technology (IT) professionals. Engaging with many corporate customers each month, the paucity of knowledge around this subject is worrying, as it will impact how we design, build, and deploy IT solutions for years to come.

Searching the Internet for sensible information is time-consuming and often shrouded in marketing speak that frustrates technical decision makers. The range of Microsoft server products, now marketed as .NET Enterprise Servers, has grown considerably over the past year, and many IT architects are struggling to find out how these products work, and are integrated, and what impact they may have on their businesses.

The importance of .NET to Microsoft cannot be underestimated. As Microsoft is the world's largest software company, this in turn makes .NET important to anyone working within IT.

This book will give you an excellent insight into .NET and how it will affect you and your business in the coming years. This is not a developer's guide, containing pages of code and systemwide settings. Rather, it has been designed for the busy IT professional who needs to learn quickly about .NET, key technologies, and products that make up a .NET solution.

- Chapter 1: Introducing .NET. Where it has come from and the core architecture

- Chapter 2: eXtensible Markup Language (XML.) What is it, how does it work, and what is its importance in today's IT systems

- Chapter 3: Visual Studio.NET. Building .NET solutions

- Chapter 4: Microsoft BizTalk Server. What is it, how does it work, and what is its importance?

- Chapter 5: Microsoft Commerce Server. What is it, how does it work, and what is its importance in building consumer Web sites

- Chapter 6: Microsoft SQL Server. The data storage product used in most .NET solutions

- Chapter 7: Microsoft Content Management Server. How to manage a Web site and ensure that the content is up-to-date and accurate.

- Chapter 8: Microsoft Application Center Server. Managing and scaling a solution

- Chapter 9: SOAP Web Services, and UDDI. A new way of building and deploying distributed solutions using SOAP and introducing UDDI and GXA.

- Chapter 10: Security and Scalability. Making .NET secure and scalable to meet enterprise requirements

- Chapter 11: Microsoft SharePoint Portal Server. Managing documents and information repositories with a Portal front end

- Glossary: A shorthand guide to the key .NET technologies and products

- Appendix: A guide to Microsoft .NET product system requirements

Acknowledgments

Writing a book can be a thankless task at times as it entails many hours of research and typing. This has inevitable effects on those closest to you and I would like to thank Rue Stanley for putting up with this for the third time.

There have been a number of colleagues involved in preparing this text, but I would like especially to thank my reviewing team of Ken England and Mark Hirst. Ken was able to bring his real-life experience of speaking to IT professionals on a daily basis and Mark has a wealth of in-depth technical knowledge on Microsoft .NET. Using feedback from them both, I hope I have tuned the book for the right IT professional audience.

I would like to thank the team at Digital Press, including Theron R. Shreve and Pam Chester, for their support of the project. In addition, a big thank you to the folks at ICS Solutions (www.ics-solutions.co.uk) who have worked so tirelessly to help Microsoft put .NET on the map in the U.K.

About the Author

Nigel Stanley is a leading expert in the field of .NET technologies and their impact on businesses. By working with many organizations across the spectrum of market sectors, he has gained a wealth of knowledge and experience, documented for the first time in this book. His other books include the two best-selling SQL Server handbooks, written with Ken England, available from Digital Press.

Introducing .NET

One thing can be said about Microsoft: It never stands still. The rate at which new products and technologies are churned out from the Redmond production mill never ceases to amaze.

As with all companies, Microsoft's ideas come and go in distinct waves. Client/server was done thoroughly for many years, from the early days of Microsoft LAN Manager to Windows NT. At that time I was working as a product manager at Microsoft U.K., responsible for the evolving Structured Query Language (SQL) Server RDBMS product on both Windows NT and OS/2. Innovation in those days was relatively slow as new features were added and improved, but because SQL Server was never seen as mainstream, this was a quiet backwater filled with database and developer tool enthusiasts.

The launch of Windows NT in August 1993 started to wedge open the corporate door for Microsoft as it started to transition from the desktop to the server. Gradually the snowball started to gather pace, as Windows NT encroached further and further into the traditional systems' glass house.

At about this time, the Internet was starting to evolve from the world of academia to the world of commerce. Little by little, organizations started to realize the potential of the Internet and World Wide Web for commercial purposes. But Microsoft was nowhere to be seen.

As an organization Microsoft may be seen as visionary, but the Internet passed it by until the well-documented Internet strategy day on December 7, 1995, when Bill Gates announced: We're [Microsoft] hard-core about the Internet. A whole new Microsoft era had begun.

Windows DNA was version 1 of Microsoft's Internet strategy. This cringingly awful acronym, standing for Distributed iNternet Architecture, was really no more than a rehash of multitier client/server computing, where the user interface layer was separated from the middle-tier business objects and the back-end database. Unfortunately for Microsoft, Windows DNA was a failure, since neither the marketing spin masters nor the technical developers really understood what Microsoft was trying to do with it.

In parallel with the Windows DNA effort, a group of senior Microsoft types was given the task of redefining the future of Windows on a project called Next Generation Windows Services, or NGWS. This was seen in the market as a strategic comeback following the U.S. Department of Justice investigation and court case. By moving the strategy forward into the future, the relevance of any legal findings would quickly fade into the annals of computing history, leaving Microsoft a clear direction ahead.

NGWS was finally renamed .NET (pronounced "dot net") and launched in June 2000.

1.1   .NET Evolves

After the launch of .NET, Microsoft appeared to enter a phase of frantic development work, while on the outside developers started to discuss what .NET was all about.

It also seemed that no one at Microsoft, apart from a select few who actually "got it," understood what .NET actually was and how it was going to change the way Microsoft did things. Lots of different views and ideas were heard as the messages from Redmond became changed in a game of Chinese whispers, no doubt reflecting the frantic efforts going on at Redmond to start shipping product.

1.2   What Is Microsoft .NET?

.NET is a set of Microsoft-based technologies that can be used to connect systems, devices, and people, using the Internet or an intranet as a backbone. .NET is being embraced by a range of Microsoft products, which makes the design, development, and deployment of solutions a lot easier than it had been in the past.

A lot of .NET functionality is facilitated through Extensible Markup Language (XML) Web services. These are small, reusable applications or pieces of code written in XML that allow data to be sent between otherwise disconnected sources (see Figure 1.1).

Microsoft has a number of server-based products that have been cobranded as .NET Enterprise Servers. These products perform various

Figure 1.1
XML Web services.

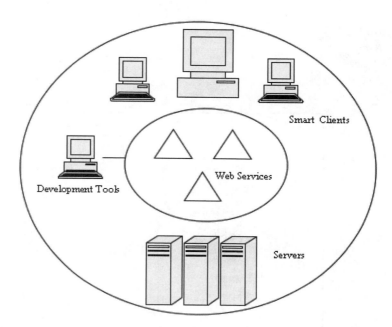

tasks—from database management with SQL Server to business-to-business messaging with BizTalk Server. In reality the amount of ".NETness" in these products has varied due to the product release cycles being out of phase with the launch of .NET. Within a couple of years all of the servers will be fully .NET with associated XML-based Web services features (see Figure 1.2).

The current .NET Enterprise Server products include the following:

- Microsoft SQL Server 2000—a relational database product

- Microsoft BizTalk Server 2002—a business-to-business messaging product

- Microsoft Commerce Server 2002—a Web site retailing product, updating Microsoft Site Server

- Microsoft Internet Security and Acceleration Server—an Internet firewall product that supports caching to improve the delivery of site pages, updating Microsoft Proxy Server

- Microsoft Application Center Server—a support product used for scaling out and managing a solution across multiple servers

- Microsoft Content Management Server—a Web site content manager that uses a database-driven content approach

Figure 1.2
.NET Enterprise Servers —a logical view.

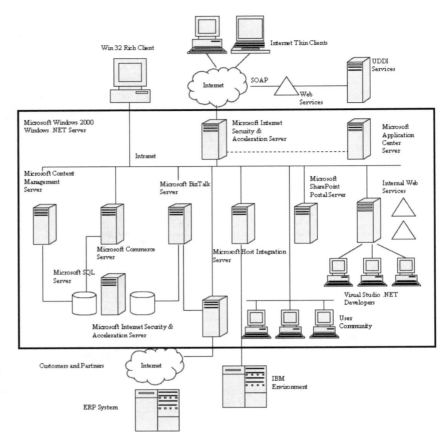

- Microsoft Host Integration Server—the Update to SNA Server that provides access to the world of IBM SNA

- Microsoft SharePoint Portal Server—document management and portal solution that permits searching and sharing of documents and other assets

- Microsoft Windows 2000 Server, Advanced Server, and Datacenter Server—a server-based platform for deploying .NET solutions

- Microsoft Project Server—a product used to share project-related and resource information

- Microsoft Operations Manager—a provider of system management tools across the enterprise

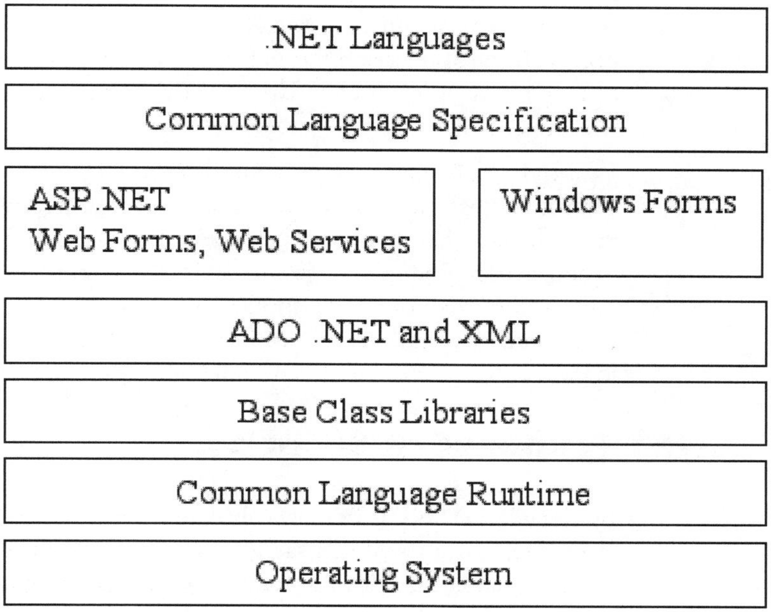

Figure 1.3
The .NET framework.

| .NET Languages |
| Common Language Specification |

| ASP .NET
Web Forms, Web Services | Windows Forms |

| ADO .NET and XML |
| Base Class Libraries |
| Common Language Runtime |
| Operating System |

1.3   .NET Framework

The .NET Framework is the environment in which a developer will design, build, and deploy a .NET-based solution. The solution can be for a Web application or rich Windows client application, because the .NET Framework encompasses access to all of the developer technologies from Microsoft, including ActiveX Template Library (ATL), COM, Microsoft Foundation Classes (MFC), and Win 32. In addition, the .NET Framework supports a number of third-party languages that have been written to conform to the Common Language Specification, a set of rules that defines how a language will perform and act within .NET. These include COBOL, Eiffel, SmallTalk, and Perl (see Figure 1.3).

Microsoft has released a lighter version of the .NET Framework called the .NET Compact Framework, designed for devices such as mobile telephones and even televisions.

1.4   Component Object Model (COM) and .NET

COM components can be accessed from the .NET Framework by using a run-time-callable wrapper, or RCW. This will take the COM interfaces and turn them into .NET Framework–compatible interfaces. Any OLE auto-mation interface can have the RCW generated automatically from a type library. If the application has non-OLE automation interfaces, it is possible to map the types exposed in the COM interface across to the .NET Framework manually.

.NET Framework components also can be used from a COM program. Managed types built within the framework can be configured, usually auto-matically, so that they can be accessed by a COM application. As you would expect, though, there are some .NET Framework features that are outside the scope of COM applications, and if you intend to have a .NET Framework application accessed from a COM application, it is probably best to decide this up front and then design out features that are inaccessible.

1.5   .NET Framework Security

By default the .NET Framework comes with security out of the box, so most applications will run safely and securely. By using the standard class libraries that come with the framework, access to resources and operations will be conducted in a secure manner, because the Framework will automat-ically enforce the appropriate security levels. If, on the other hand, you are writing a set of new base class libraries for your application that expose new resources, then you will need to understand the security system in more detail. Luckily, only the code that overrides the security system will need to be closely monitored, because the rest of the code will run happily in the context of the framework security model.

1.6   ASP.NET

ASP.NET is the next stage in the evolution of Microsoft Web-development technology. Essentially it is the coming together of Active Server Pages (ASP) and the Common Language Runtime (CLR) with some extra good-ies added on. The end result is a fairly comprehensive environment for building Web-based applications.

Web Forms are at the core of applications written within ASP.NET and provide the user interface (UI) layer. In early Web development, the UI was severely limited in what it could support, and the applications were bland in the extreme. With Web Forms, a lot of the richness associated with the more traditional client/server applications has now been brought into the world of the Web.

A Web Form comprises the user interface stored in an ASPX file and a separate class file that stores the code behind the form. The user interface can have a number of objects added to it in the form of controls. These include HTML, Web Form, Field Validator, and Custom controls.

- **HTML controls.** These are designed to behave in the same way as controls added by HTML editors and include standard controls such as text areas, password fields, and buttons.
- **Web Form controls.** Like HTML controls, these can detect the type of browser reading the page and adjust its look and feel accordingly.
- **Field Validator controls.** These are used to avoid round trips when checking to see if a value has been filled into a control. In practice the control writes client-side JavaScript into the HTML page, which can be read by any browser to execute the checking process.
- **Custom controls.** These can perform any customized function.

Web Forms behave a lot like Windows Forms in that a series of events will run when the form is started and loads. In addition, events will be raised when the user interacts with the form in the browser.

1.7 ADO.NET

As its name suggests, ADO.NET is the next technology in the evolution of ADO and was released as part of the .NET Framework, the collection of technologies that supports .NET development.

ADO.NET supports typed programming. This useful feature uses a lot of end-user type words in the developer's code that are self-explanatory to anyone reading it and therefore make for easier support. It is also type-safe, since during code compilation, incorrect use of data types is picked up and reported back to the developer for remedial action, as opposed to a weakly typed environment that would report such an error at runtime only and be more difficult to track down.

While ADO may have been good enough for client/server-based development, there are some important differences between that type of development and Web-based development:

- *The Web is disconnected.* Managing applications that only connect to the database when they need data is different from the way in which client/server applications worked, when the connection was more or less open all of the time. Users of early versions of Microsoft Access and SQL Server realized this when upsizing Access to SQL Server. Very soon SQL Server ran out of connections since Access was consuming no end of connections per user for such things as keeping track of the table key. Thankfully, this connection limitation was removed from SQL Server a few years ago.

- *Web applications need to scale.* Keeping connections open to a database is expensive in terms of system resources and leads to applications collapsing with tens of users as opposed to the thousands of users of a Web application.

- *New technological innovations such as XML are changing the way applications request and receive data across the Web.* Connection technologies need to take this into account and support the use of XML.

To manage the disconnected nature of SQL Server data in a Web-based application, ADO.NET creates a data cache populated with the data the user wishes to see. Once the cache is populated, the database connection is disconnected until the user makes changes to the cached data, which is then sent back to the database server. The data is actually streamed in XML between the application and SQL Server, and if the data is required elsewhere, then again they are persisted (i.e., saved) in XML format.

1.8   The Future of .NET

.NET is a huge bet for Microsoft, one it has to win if it is to continue to dominate the world of software. One strand of this success will comprise technical innovations, which will enable Microsoft to remain ahead of the competition.

Microsoft is investing over $5 billion per year in research and development (R&D). This in turn provides innovative product features and new techniques for advancing the range of Microsoft software opportunities.

A significant player in this R&D effort is Microsoft Research. Based across five sites, including locations in Redmond, WA; Cambridge, U.K.; and Beijing, China, Microsoft Research (www.research.microsoft.com) employs over 500 people dedicated to basic and applied research in computer science. The scope of the work undertaken is huge and touches every aspect of computing, from voice recognition to graphics and database search algorithms. In parallel to this, there is a technology-transfer function whose role is to convert any useful findings into products or features for Microsoft product teams.

Microsoft is also undergoing a change in its "go-to-market" strategy as it starts to embrace a solution sales approach. This moves Microsoft sales people away from the features and benefits of individual products to focusing on business problems and how they may be addressed by a range of Microsoft products sold as a solution.

As this book is written in the autumn of 2002, Microsoft has realized the tremendous effort it still needs to put into making .NET a success. We are now entering the second phase of .NET as organizations slowly start to realize the implications of XML, Web services, and the .NET strategy for their business and information technology needs.

The most exciting phase is yet to come!

eXtensible Markup Language (XML)

XML is a core part of .NET, and all Microsoft .NET products support XML in some form or another. On that basis no, .NET project can avoid the use of XML somewhere down the line, so understanding it is extremely important.

XML is a system used to define, validate, and share document formats. It comes from the same heritage as HyperText Markup Language (HTML).

2.1 SGML

The common heritage of HTML and XML is Standardized General Markup Language (SGML), first published by the International Organization for Standardization, or ISO, in 1986.

SGML was designed to offer a hardware- and software-independent way to display text electronically in the burgeoning electronic publishing industry. Markup is a term used by typesetters referring to the annotations given to text on documents, indicating how text should be displayed, such as **bold**, *italic,* or underlined. In some respects punctuation can be thought of as a markup language since it indicates the structure of a piece of text, such as where a line should end (period) or a list of items begins (colon).

In essence HTML documents are a subset of SGML documents designed for use on the World Wide Web.

2.2 HTML

HTML is a straightforward markup language designed to create hypertext documents that are platform independent. In fact, HTML has been used on the World Wide Web as the standard markup language since 1990.

HTML at its basic level is straightforward to write, and any user with a text editor can create an HTML file. With the use of advanced tags, text can be placed around pictures, line breaks forced, and tables built.

This code segment shows some common HTML tags:

```
<html>

<head>
<meta name="GENERATOR" content="Microsoft FrontPage 5.0">
<meta name="ProgId" content="FrontPage.Editor.Document">
<meta http-equiv="Content-Type" content="text/html;
charset=windows-1252">
<title>New Page 1</title>
</head>

<body>

<h1>This is the First Heading</h1>
<h2>This is the Second Heading</h2>
<p>This is the first Paragraph.</p>
<p>
<img SRC="file:///C:/DOCUME~1/server1/LOCALS~1/Temp/
FrontPageTempDir/XML.jpg" WIDTH="300" HEIGHT="250">This
a link to
<a HREF="file:///C:/DOCUME~1/server1/LOCALS~1/Temp
/FrontPageTempDir/TopShed.html">
the shed page</a>. This is a link to our company
<a HREF="http://www.ics-solutions.co.uk/a"> website </a>
</p>

</body>

</html>
```

But at the end of the day, there is little intelligence in an HTML document. All I am doing is describing how the text is to appear on the browser screen, but not actually describing the data. This is where XML comes to the fore.

2.3   **XML**

XML makes it easy for a computer to describe, read, and generate data. It uses a structure of tags in a manner similar to HTML, but in this case the tags can be fully customized to suit a particular self-describing requirement. The concept of customizing tags enables a common definition of entities or documents to be created—such as invoices—that in turn allows organizations to transfer data relatively easily. Indeed, there is a Web site, (www.biztalk.org) designed to act as a community library for organizations to share these common document types.

An interesting point to note is that if you see a tag in XML such as `<p>` it can refer to anything—but it will not indicate a new paragraph!

Here is an example of some simple XML code:

```
<?xml version="1.0">
<Library>
    <Book>
        <Title>Biography of Colonel Stephens</Title>
        <Author>John Scott Morgan</Author>
    </Book>
    <Picture>
        <Title>Fishermen</Title>
        <Artist>J R Hartley</Artist>
    </Picture>
</Library>
```

How is the code structured? The first line declares the version of XML being used and acts as a processing instruction. This is an attribute, because it takes the form of `name="value"`. While not strictly needed, it is a good practice to include this statement.

The tag `<Library>` is called the enclosing element, which all XML documents must have irrespective of whether they contain the processing instruction. There are two subelements, indicated by the `</Book>` and `</Picture>` tags.

In fact, the tags act as data delimiters, and the application reading the XML will need to interpret the specific data. Interestingly, by simply reading the XML code the chances are you could work out what the XML file was referring to. This is the real beauty of XML—the fact that it is self-describing.

Now, an XML document needs to be well-formed and valid. By well-formed we are ensuring that the document can be read by a program and transmitted across a network. Specifically, a well-formed piece of XML has the following:

- All of the document's begin and end tags matching
- Quotes around attribute values
- Entities such as macros declared
- All empty tags defined as <empty/>

By valid we are ensuring that the piece of XML has a document type definition, or DTD. The DTD describes which tags can be used and which nesting levels are permitted within the XML document. In addition, the DTD declares entities, which are pieces of text that can be reused in the XML document, but only need to be sent across the network once. The document validity also ensures that tags are ordered properly, making them easier to reuse when needed.

Staying with our library theme, here is a simple DTD used to describe a book library:

```
<!ELEMENT Library (Book*)>
<!ELEMENT Book ( Title, Author*, Copyright )>
<!ELEMENT Title (#PCDATA)>
<!ELEMENT Author (#PCDATA)>
<!ELEMENT Copyright (#PCDATA)>
```

The simple elements are represented by the element name followed by the contents, in this case described as character data. In this case, the element `Title` will have character data:

```
<!ELEMENT Title (#PCDATA)>
```

Elements can also contain other elements, and if they can have zero or more elements, then the element is followed by an asterisk (*):

```
<!ELEMENT Book ( Title, Author*, Copyright )>
```

This would tell us that the book element can have one title, many authors (i.e., coauthors), and one copyright owner.

Using a DTD is quite straightforward, as the following code segment shows:

```
<?xml version="1.0" ?>
<!DOCTYPE Library PUBLIC "." "Library.dtd" >
<Library>
    <Book>
        <Title>The Road Ahead</Title>
        <Author>Bill Gates</Author>
        <Copyright>1998</Copyright>
    </Book>
    <Book>
        <Title>Trainspotters Ball</Title>
        <Author>Stanley</Author>
        <Copyright>2001</Copyright>
    </Book>
</Library>
```

The XML parser, probably your browser in most instances, will load the DTD "Library.dtd" and then use it to validate the rest of the document. As you may realize, DTDs are rather limited because they define the element structure and the nature of the data allowed in each of the elements. This limitation is another example of SGML's influence on XML, and something had to be done to improve this for better use across the Internet.

In place of a DTD, an XML author can use an XML schema. In fact, this is fast becoming the most appropriate technique, especially since Simple Object Access Protocol (SOAP) see Chapter 9 specifically says that a SOAP message must not contain a DTD.

2.3.1   XML Schemata

XML schemata are supersets of DTDs. Although they are both used to structure an XML document, only the XML schema is capable of providing type information.

Here is the same library example, but represented as an XML schema:

```
<schema xmlns:xsd=
"http://www.w3.org/2001/XMLSchema"
    targetNamespace=
        "http://www.testnamespace.com/LibrarySchema.xml"
    xmlns:xsi=
        "http://www.w3.org/2001/XMLSchema-instance">
    <complexType name="Book">
        <element type="Title"></element>
        <element type="Author"></element>
        <element type="Copyright"></element>
    </complexType>
    <simpleType name="Title" xsi:type="string">
    </simpleType>
    <simpleType name="Author" xsi:type="string">
    </simpleType>
    <simpleType name="Copyright" xsi:type="integer">
    </simpleType>
</schema>
```

The schema is another XML file, and to use it, the appropriate namespace is referenced in the document as follows:

```
<myLibrary:Library xmlns:myLibrary=
    "http://www.testnamespace.com/LibrarySchema.xml">
    <myLibrary:Book>
        <myLibrary:Title>GER Y4 at Stratford
        </myLibrary:Title>
        <myLibrary:Author>Doug Hewson
        </myLibrary:Author>
        <myLibrary:Copyright>1991
        </myLibrary:Copyright>
    </myLibrary:Book>
    <myLibrary:Book>
        <myLibrary:Title>Growler Confessions
        </myLibrary:Title>
        <myLibrary:Author>Dan Jeavons
        </myLibrary:Author>
        <myLibrary:Copyright>2001
        </myLibrary:Copyright>
    </myLibrary:Book>
</myLibrary:Library>
```

Note the line of text that reads

```
<myLibrary:Library xmlns:myLibrary=
    "http://www.testnamespace.com/LibrarySchema.xml">
```

This is a unique value that can be used to tell the parser to use the set of names defined and identified in the following URI location. All of the elements contained within the `xmlns` tags are part of the specified namespace unless explicitly stated otherwise.

2.3.2 XML Namespaces

A namespace allows a given set of unique names to be used within a given context. This is used to prevent the names of elements clashing within a document. In the `Mylibrary` example, we have an element called `title`, which in this instance is a book title.

In another context this could be a person's title, such as Mr., Mrs., or Ms. All of this could be quite confusing, so by using the `libraryschema.xml` namespace, we are saying: that in our example `title` means a book title.

This technique has been used for a while in C++, and, while sometimes seen as an unfortunate overhead, this is the way the World Wide Web Consortium (W3C) has determined it will work.

2.3.3 XML API

XML is only useful if you can do something with it. Programmatic access to XML or a piece of software that is capable of reading an XML document is called an XML API or, more often, an XML processor.

Currently there are two commonly used XML processors that are gaining acceptance: the document object model, or DOM, and the Simple API for XML, or SAX.

DOM

The DOM is an internal tree structure, which is built to represent an XML document. When the XML processor loads the XML document, it builds an in-memory tree, which can then be programmatically accessed or traversed using the names of the methods defined in the DOM.

SAX

Imagine loading a large XML document into memory. This overhead is one of the significant downsides of using the DOM approach, and it led to a group of developers joining together to define a new approach.

With SAX the XML processor, after reading each element in the XML document, calls a custom event handler to just-in-time process the element and data. While it does offer improved performance, it does limit a developer's flexibility and needs to be assessed alongside the DOM approach.

2.3.4 Transforming XML

Traversing the DOM tree to extract elements can be both tedious and time consuming, reading each element and then building, for example, an HTML document. This is probably the most frequently needed transformation—taking XML data and turning these data into HTML for users to view.

To improve the efficiency of transforming XML documents, the W3C introduced a specification for XML transformations called the Extensible Stylesheet Language, or XSL, and a simple query language called XSL Patterns.

Using XSL, developers now have the ability to perform complex transformations. A good example is receiving an XML document that does not support the vocabulary of your own XML document. By using an XSL transformation, you can turn the XML document into something that your document will understand (See Figure 2.1).

Here is an example of transforming an XML file. We take the base XML file:

```
<?xml version="1.0"?>
<Books>
  <Book cheap="Afraid not">
    <name>Picture Book</name>
    <description>Gold embossed with nice writing.</
description>
    <price>1000</price>
  </Book>
</Books>
```

and we transform it into this HTML file for our users to view:

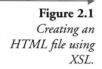

Figure 2.1
*Creating an
HTML file using
XSL.*

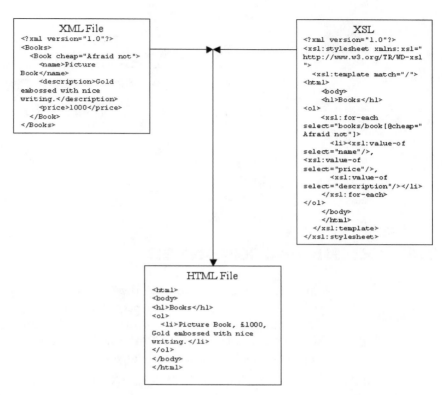

```
<html>
<body>
<h1>Books</h1>
<ol>
   <li>Picture Book, £1000, Gold embossed with nice
writing.</li>
</ol>
</body>
</html>
```

So, we apply the following XSL file:

```
<?xml version="1.0"?>
<xsl:stylesheet xmlns:xsl=" http://www.w3.org/TR/WD-xsl">
   <xsl:template match="/">
<html>
```

```
        <body>
        <h1>Books</h1>
<ol>
        <xsl:for-each select="books/book[@cheap="Afraid not"]>
           <li><xsl:value-of select="name"/>, <xsl:value-of
select="price"/>,
           <xsl:value-of select="description"/></li>
        </xsl:for-each>
</ol>
        </body>
        </html>
    </xsl:template>
</xsl:stylesheet>
```

2.4   **XLINK and XPOINTER**

Chances are, each time you visit the Web and find a page that interests you, you will find a link to another page that might be even more interesting. This linking of pages is one of the more compelling aspects of the Web. With the transition to using XML for data description on the Web, a new way of linking XML documents together is needed.

XML Linking, or XLINK, is a W3C standard that defines the syntax with which XML documents can be linked on the Web. XLINK allows specific relationships to be created between resources, accompanied by some descriptive data.

This is an example of a simple XLINK:

```
<book xml:link="simple"
HREF = "http://kenslibrary.org/book.htm">
</book>
```

XPOINTER, another W3C standard, specifies the way in which specific elements can be referenced within an XML document, whether or not they contain an explicit identifier. For example:

```
child(3,book)
```

This will refer to the third child element whose type is book.

2.5   XML in Microsoft SQL Server 2000

Microsoft SQL Server 2000 ships with a number of XML features in the box, making the process of turning relational data into XML reasonably straightforward.

2.5.1   Data Access from a URL

Transact SQL (T-SQL) statements can now be submitted directly to SQL Server from a Web site URL (uniform resource location—the *www* address of a Web site), since SQL Server ships with a set of SQL Internet Server API (ISAPI) extensions. A typical use of this would be to submit a query or execute a stored procedure as part of the Web site address.

A typical example could be

```
http://IISServer/
pubs?sql=SELECT+*+FROM+Authors+FOR+XML+RAW&root=root
```

By using FOR XML RAW, we are actually returning the customer's data as an XML document rather than a SQL Server record set. This will be explained later.

To overcome the problem of limited character space in a URL, and the security risk of allowing direct query access to SQL Server, the better way to implement this is to use XML templates. The templates are used to store the T-SQL statements and XPATH queries. For example:

```
http://IISServer/pubs/Templates/templatefile.xml
```

This has the added benefit of securing the detail of the T-SQL statements, thereby providing a layer of basic security.

A typical template file would look like this:

```
<ROOT xmlns:sql="urn:schemas-microsoft-com:xml-sql">
    <sql:query>
      SELECT   *
      FROM     Authors
      FOR XML RAW
    </sql:query>
</ROOT>
```

Note the use of the namespace.

The T-SQL SELECT statement has now been extended to include additional keywords in support of three XML modes that determine the nature or serialization of the retrieved XML data.

RAW

RAW takes each row returned from the query and places it within a generic element tag <row/>. For example, this RAW output has au_lname and title contained in the <row/> tags.

```
<?xml version="1.0" ?>
<ROOT>
  <row au_lname="England" title="The SQL Server Magical
Database Guide" />
  <row au_lname="Blotchet-Halls" title="Fifty Years in
Buckingham Palace Kitchens" />
  <row au_lname="Carson" title="But Is It User Friendly?" />
  <row au_lname="DeFrance" title="The Gourmet Microwave" />
</ROOT>
```

This is the most basic form of output with limited use.

AUTO

AUTO builds what is called a nested XML tree with XML elements built from the tables included in the SELECT statement.

```
<?xml version="1.0" ?>
<ROOT>
<authors au_lname="England">
  <titles title="The SQL Server Magical Database Guide" />
</authors>
<authors au_lname="Blotchet-Halls">
  <titles title="Fifty Years in Buckingham Palace Kitchens" />
</authors>
<authors au_lname="Carson">
  <titles title="But Is It User Friendly?" />
</authors>
<authors au_lname="DeFrance">
  <titles title="The Gourmet Microwave" />
</authors>
</ROOT>
```

EXPLICIT

EXPLICIT is more complicated, but allows the query to specify the appropriate XML nesting and the precise nature of the XML structure. This is far more useful to the developer, although the understanding required of XML is a bit deeper.

2.6   SQLXML

With the fast pace of change around XML, and Microsoft realized that SQL Server XML functionality would soon be out of date unless it released update packs with enhanced XML functionality prior to the release of YUKON, the next full version of the product expected by the end of 2003. SQLXML is a free-of-charge download that includes some new XML functionality, including the ability to expose stored procedures as Web services via SOAP. SQLXML 3.0 also updates support of Diffgrams, which allow data updates via XML data sets.

2.7   XQL—XML Query Language

Just when you thought there were no other XML derivatives, another appears called XML Query Language, or XQL.

XQL is very similar to XSL Patterns. It uses XML as its data model and XPath as the language to create expressions or manipulate numbers and strings. The useful part of XQL is its versatility, as it can be used to build expressions as part of a URL, XML, or HTML object. For example, here is an XPath query that will search for bookstores that have a legal speciality:

```
/bookstore[@specialty = "legal"]
```

Or, in this example, the query will search for every XML element that is called code.

```
//author
```

As you no doubt can see, XML has revolutionized the way that data is managed across the Internet. Innovations around XML are set to continue, all designed to make the sharing of data easier than it has ever been.

Visual Studio.NET

3.1   What Is Visual Studio.NET?

Visual Studio.NET is a development environment that acts as the host for the range of Microsoft .NET languages such as Visual Basic, C++ and C#. The objective behind Visual Studio is to have a single interface and set of tools that work across any .NET language irrespective of the language's features or semantics. This type of development tool is often referred to as an Integrated Development Environment, or IDE (See Figure 3.1).

Figure 3.1
Visual Studio .NET showing the startup wizard and basic IDE.

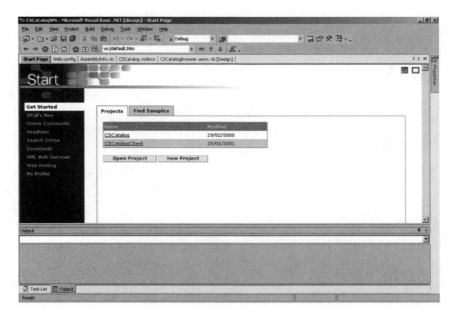

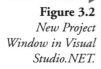

Figure 3.2
*New Project
Window in Visual
Studio.NET.*

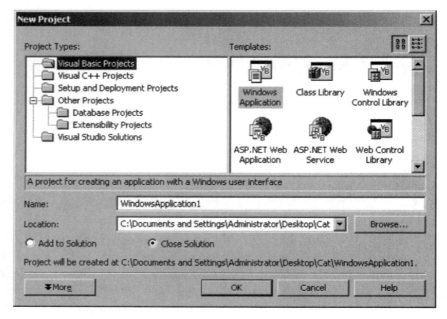

3.2 What You Get with Visual Studio.NET

Within the Visual Studio IDE, there are tools to assist the developer, including the following:

- The help system is dynamic and context sensitive. Using IntelliSense Visual Studio will offer relevant code hints and, where appropriate, auto complete lines of code (see Figure 3.2).

- The Solution Explorer contains all of the related files used by a specific project, and the toolbox has been extended to include all the items a developer is likely to need when writing an application (see Figure 3.3).

- The Server Explorer lists all of the server-based resources used by a project, including databases, message queues, and event logs (see Figure 3.4).

- The Task List Explorer allows developers to maintain a list of things to do; this can be commented and then accessed by other team members, giving better support for multiperson development teams.

Figure 3.3
Solution Explorer window.

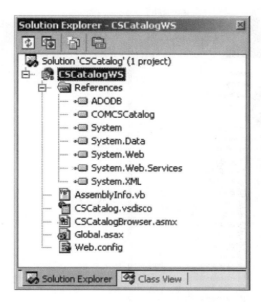

- The debugging of code has been extended in Visual Studio.NET with support for cross-language debugging for development teams using different languages in a project.

- The Forms Designer now allows both traditional Windows forms and forms for Web-based applications to be created using the usual drag-and-drop design format.

- The XML Designer allows XML schema and data files to be created and edited. IntelliSense statement completion is available, if you are writing XML based on a known schema.

3.3   Visual Studio.NET Varieties

Visual Studio.NET is available in four versions:

1.   Professional

2.   Enterprise Developer

3.   Enterprise Architect

4.   Academic

Figure 3.4
Server Explorer window.

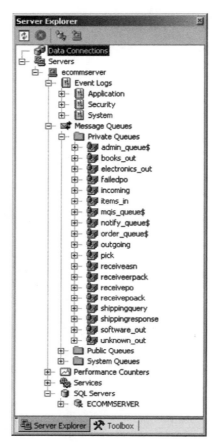

All versions contain the development environment; one or more languages, such as Visual Basic, C++, and C#; and tools to support building and developing for the SQL Server desktop engine. Enterprise Developer and Architect have additional support for the full version of SQL Server, Oracle, SourceSafe, and other .NET Enterprise Server products. Enterprise Architect also includes Visio design tools. The Academic product is the same specification as Visual Studio Professional, but includes some help and solution examples tailored for academia.

3.4   Microsoft .NET Languages

Language choice is probably one of the most contentious debates among developers from whatever background. Partly fueled by fear (i.e., my language must be in demand, because I need a job) and partly fueled by dislikes for language deficiencies (i.e., my language has better semantics), many hours have been spent arguing the importance of different languages. Professional developers have often besmirched, those they consider amateurs, for using "toy" languages, such as Visual Basic.

In all this, it is important to remember that code is written to build solutions for organizations and businesses. Most business people I speak to don't know one end of Visual C++ from the other, and why should they? It has no bearing on the solution, other than the likely elapsed time to write the code and possible postdevelopment support concerns. Certainly Visual C++ has been held to be the superior development language for building packaged software applications, and Microsoft uses it for most of its development work.

The problem is that it takes most people two to three years to reach a proficient level of skill in Visual C++, which in turn leads to a more costly skills shortage.

Languages like Visual Basic, on the other hand, can be picked up by most IT literate and motivated individuals within a couple of weeks, and certainly within a year, one would expect a developer to have become quite proficient in Visual Basic development. The reason for this is that the development environment and language remove the need for the developer to get involved in complex problems, such as memory management (although the Common Language Runtime [CLR] in Visual Studio .NET has removed this for managed code written in Visual C++ as well). The end result is that there are lots of developers writing Visual Basic code (6 million worldwide according to Microsoft), but there also a lot of dreadful applications with spaghetti code and atrocious performance.

This language debate has now been halted with the release of Visual Studio.NET and its support for language interoperability.

Language interoperability is the ability for a piece of code to interact fully with another piece of code, irrespective of the programming languages used. The end result is maximum reuse of code but, more importantly, maximum reuse of developer expertise.

Visual C++ developers can now work proactively alongside Visual Basic colleagues on the same project, sharing chunks of code to be written, in the knowledge that the CLR will pull the solution together.

Each language that targets the CLR needs to follow some strict rules that permit this interchange of code. These rules are defined in the Common Language Specification, or CLS.

The CLS has a common type system that puts in place a set of rules defining the types that a programmer can use, ensuring type consistency across all languages. A set of metadata rules enables language interoperability by defining a uniform way for storing and retrieving information about these types. Compilers store type information as metadata, which the CLR then uses to provide services during execution. Without this it would be impossible to read values into and out of the memory stack, and types would be overwritten in the heap, leading to program crashes.

The level of code interoperability is tremendous. Types can inherit implementation from other types, pass objects to another type's methods, and call methods defined by other types. Exception handling is now consistent and exceptions raised in one language can be trapped and dealt with by an object written in another language.

The following examples carry out the exact same task, selecting data from a SQL Server database, but they are written in different CLS-compatible languages:

- Visual Basic.NET

```
Dim s as String
s = "loconumbers"
Dim cmd As New SqlCommand("select * from " & s, sqlconn)
cmd.ExecuteReader()
```

- C#

```
string s = "loconumbers";
SqlCommand cmd = new SqlCommand("select * from "+s,
sqlconn);
cmd.ExecuteReader();
```

- Visual C++

```
String *s = S"loconumbers";
SqlCommand cmd = new SqlCommand(String::Concat
(S"select * from ", s),sqlconn);
cmd.ExecuteReader();
```

- J#

```
String s = "loconumbers";
```

```
SqlCommand cmd = new SqlCommand("select * from "+s,
sqlconn);
cmd.ExecuteReader();
```

- ## COBOL

```
ENVIRONMENT DIVISION.
CONFIGURATION SECTION.
REPOSITORY.
    CLASS SqlCommand AS
"System.Data.SqlClient.SqlCommand"
    CLASS SqlConnection AS
"System.Data.SqlClient.SqlConnection".
DATA DIVISION.
WORKING-STORAGE SECTION.
01 str PIC X(50).
01 cmd-string PIC X(50).
01 cmd OBJECT REFERENCE SqlCommand.
01 sqlconn OBJECT REFERENCE SqlConnection.
PROCEDURE DIVISION.
 *> Establish the SQL connection.
MOVE "loconumbers" TO str.
STRING "select * from " DELIMITED BY SIZE,
    str DELIMITED BY " " INTO cmd-string.
INVOKE SqlCommand "NEW" USING BY VALUE cmd-string sqlconn
RETURNING cmd.
INVOKE cmd "ExecuteReader".
```

- ## Mondrian

```
ExecuteReader = invoke
System.Data.SqlClient.ExecuteReader();
SqlCommand = create
System.Data.SqlClient.SqlCommand(String,\
                 System.Data.SqlClient.SqlConnection);
query = sqlconn -> let{ s = "loconumbers"; } in {
   cmd <- SqlCommand ("select * from "+s, sqlconn);
   cmd # ExecuteReader();
};
```

3.5 Visual Basic.NET

Visual Basic, or VBC is rumored to be Bill Gates' most popular development tool, and on that basis has achieved a lot of focus from Microsoft since it was released as version 1 in 1991. Visual Basic 3.0 introduced Data Access Objects, or DAO—which made the creation of database applications easier than before, although performance was an issue.

With Windows 95, Microsoft released Visual Basic 4.0, and for the first time, Microsoft VB developers had a 32-bit development environment. VB 5.0 introduced ActiveX control authoring for fledgling Internet development, and finally VB 6.0 introduced Web Classes and ActiveX/DHTML development.

Since then, it has been a very barren period between VB 6 and Visual Basic.NET. The reason for this is that it has taken Microsoft a long time to get the development environment right for building Web-based applications, and bringing Visual Basic up-to-date with modern features worthy of a decent development language has been time consuming. Finally, on January 13, 2002, developers could breathe a sigh of relief as Microsoft finally launched Visual Studio.NET and the latest version of Visual Basic.

3.5.1 Inheritance

A major gripe of Visual Basic developers in the past has been the lack of inheritance. Since most new development work relies on reusing code, this has been a stumbling block for Microsoft. By using a new keyword, `inherits`, functionality can be reused from a base class in other subsequent classes.

3.5.2 Free Threading

Creating any application capable of scaling to support many users in Visual Basic has been difficult in the past since Visual Basic code is executed synchronously—each line of code being executed in turn.

VB.NET supports free threading, a technique that enables a piece of code to go away and run while allowing other code to execute concurrently. This is very useful if you have some code that needs to run a complex query or process, because it can be spawned off from the main application, allowing the main code to continue executing.

3.5.3 **Error Handling**

Error handling in Visual Basic has traditionally been reliant on the statement On Error GOTO, which has caused problems for large-scale applications, as well as maintenance headaches, since the GOTO statement leads to spaghetti code. VB.NET has introduced a new error trapping mechanism called Try...Catch..Finally, which provides a structured way of dealing with code errors.

Type checking historically has been fairly lax in Visual Basic, and developers have more or less been given a free hand when it comes to correct use of data types. With the advent of VB.NET and especially the CLR, which is covered later in this chapter, type checking is a crucial part of VB.NET development and is a new discipline that developers will need to learn.

3.6 Upgrading from Visual Basic 6 to Visual Basic.NET

Due to the significant changes Microsoft put in place with VB.NET, existing VB applications need to be upgraded to work in the new environ-

Figure 3.5
Visual Basic upgrade wizard.

Figure 3.6
Once upgraded, a task list appears, and the code that needs changing is highlighted.

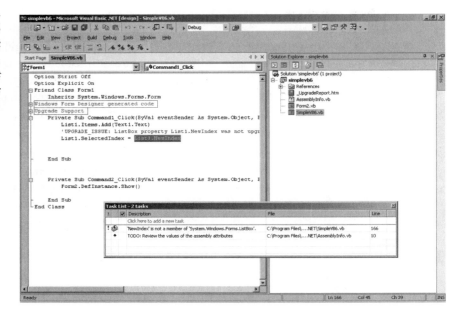

ment. Microsoft has created an upgrade tool that uses wizards to take an application through the upgrade process. The original VB project remains unaltered, and a new version is created that has areas upgraded where appropriate. (See Figure 3.5)

As you would expect, it is not possible to guarantee that 100 percent of an application will be upgraded by running a simple wizard tool, and any areas that need attention are highlighted in the new application; they then need to be edited or changed by hand. A rather neat task list is automatically created so that you can see the scope of the work that needs to be completed (see Figure 3.6).

3.7   C# (Pronounced "See Sharp")

Anders Hejlsberg, the creator of Borland's Delphi development language, was given the task by Microsoft to come up with a brand new development language from scratch. For many software engineers this is the chance of a lifetime—to do away with all of those irritating problems that other languages have and to create something completely revolutionary. The goal was to bridge the gap between the innate power of C++ and the relative ease of use of Visual Basic.

In June 2000 Microsoft announced C#.

Since C# has been written to the CLS, it can use all of the IDE features available to other .NET languages, such as Visual Basic. This has a distinct advantage in that only one IDE needs to be learned.

In an effort to gain widespread acceptance for C#, the language was submitted to the European Computer Manufacturers Association (ECMA) for ratification as an open standard. Thus, Microsoft has not only created a brand new, modern development language from scratch, but it has released intellectual property out into the public domain.

C# is gaining a lot of mind share with professional developers, and there are moves afoot to ensure that it remains ahead of the game in terms of innovations. A number of traditional Visual Basic developers are now moving directly to C# rather than upgrading to Visual Basic.NET, and the once popular Visual Basic product appears to be succumbing to the more modern C#.

3.8   Visual C++

Over recent years, C++ has been the language of choice for developers writing packaged applications or solutions that need C++'s extra performance. In fact, C++ is used to write many of the applications that Microsoft releases and is the staple tool of the Redmond-based developers.

As expected, Visual C++ has undergone some enhancements for .NET, but one of the major differences between it and the other .NET languages is the support for both managed and unmanaged code.

Managed code is written when C++ classes need to use the .NET Framework. Visual C++ now has a set of extensions to the language that enables developers to target the .NET platform with their application.

3.9   Introducing the CLR

Simply put, the CLR is a high-performance program execution engine. Any code that is designed or targeted to run within the CLR is called "managed code" and as such benefits from a number of built-in services that make the developer's life a bit easier. During the development phase, the CLR automates a number of tasks and prevents the developer from worrying about such things as cross-language exception handling, dynamic binding, and reflection (Reflection is the process by which a program can read its own metadata). During the execution phase the CLR manages, among others, application memory, garbage collection, security enforcement, and thread management.

Microsoft provides a core set of languages that target the CLR, and developers can decide to use one of these or a third-party language/compiler such as COBOL or Eiffel. In fact, the designers of the CLR decided to target up to 20 languages outside of the Microsoft fold, making the CLR a pretty versatile multilanguage engine.

By using a specific language compiler, you are agreeing to use the prescribed syntax that comes with that language. In addition, your chosen compiler determines which runtime features are available. To allow component reuse across languages and compilers, any exported types must adhere to language features included in the CLS.

During compilation, the source code is translated into a CPU-independent set of instructions called the Microsoft Intermediate Language, or MSIL. This in turn can easily be converted into native code. Typically the MSIL will contain a range of instructions to load, store, and initialize objects and undertake logical or mathematical operations. Prior to execution, the MSIL needs to be converted to CPU-specific code, and this is done by the Just-In-Time, or JIT compiler in the CLR. Different JIT compilers are available for different CPU architectures, allowing the same MSIL to be deployed on any supported chip set.

Associated with any MSIL is a set of metadata, that describes a set of types used during execution time. These metadata allow the code to be self-describing, so type libraries and Interface Description Languages, or IDLs, are no longer necessary. The CLR will read through the metadata when needed during execution.

The MSIL and metadata package are contained in a portable execution, or PE, file, which is based on the Microsoft Common Object File Format COFF, standard.

As you would expect, the JIT compiler does more than simply compile all of the code in the PE file to native code in one go. In a typical application not all of the code gets called in every execution. A good example is Word for Windows—as I write this book I probably only use about 10 percent of the available functionality, so I won't need to embed too many Excel documents into this book!

The JIT compiler actually converts the MSIL as it needs to during execution, storing the native code separately so that it is available for subsequent use. When a type is loaded, the loader creates and attaches a stub to each of its methods. When the method is first called, the stub will pass control to the

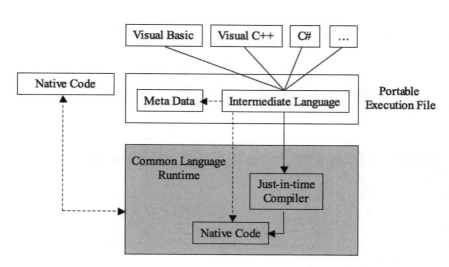

Figure 3.7
*Visual Studio and
the CLR.*

JIT compiler, which, in turn, converts the MSIL into native code and changes the stub to direct execution from the location of the native code. Any further calls to this compiled method are directed to the native code.

What happens if you do want the whole application compiled? In this case there is another compilation mode called install-time code generation. This converts the MSIL the same as the JIT compiler, but converts much larger chunks at a time. In fact, the entire assembly would be converted to native code resulting in much faster load and start times during execution (see Figure 3.7).

As you would expect, security is an important consideration for any application. Any code, during the MSIL to native-mode compilation, must pass through a verification process. The only exception to this would be if an administrator has built a security policy that allows code to bypass this verification process.

During verification, the MSIL and metadata is examined to see if they are type safe, ensuring that the code can only access memory areas it is permitted to. This also prevents objects from trampling each other or corrupting other memory areas, either deliberately through malicious intent or accidentally. Any security policies imposed by the administrator are also verified to ensure they are enforceable.

To pass as type safe, the following must be true:

- All identities are correct and what they claim to be.

- Any reference to a type is fully compatible with the type being referenced.

- Any operations invoked on an object are predefined and appropriate for that object.

Some languages, by design, do not produce code that is verifiably type safe. If a security policy is set up demanding type-safe code and the language does not pass verification, an error will be raised during execution.

3.10 Memory Management and the CLR

Automatic memory management is a service that you get with the CLR during managed execution. The CLR garbage collector will oversee the allocation and deallocation of memory, saving the developer having to write acres of memory management code, possibly getting it wrong, and crashing the application.

When a new process is started, the CLR puts aside a chunk of memory, which is called the managed heap. The managed heap contains a pointer, initially set at the base address, to the address where the next object in the heap will be allocated. All reference types are allocated on the managed heap, and the CLR will automatically allocate address space from the heap as long as there are enough addresses in the address space.

This process is extremely fast since the CLR manages objects consecutively in a contiguous block in the heap.

Garbage collection works by deciding the best time to take back some memory. By working in a series of generations, the garbage collector determines how recently an object has been used. When the first generation (actually generation 0) is full it will then perform what is known as a collection and release memory held by objects that are no longer being used.

Memory-collection decisions are based on an application's roots, which either contain a null or a reference to an object. An internal graph is created of objects that can be reached from these roots: any object that does not figure on this graph is considered unreachable, and its memory will be deallocated. These fragments of memory are then compacted into contiguous blocks, and the application roots are updated so that they point to the object in its new location.

Some applications, known as unmanaged, require explicit clean up of the memory. This is mostly when the unmanaged resource is wrapping around an operating system resource such as a file handle or network connection. The developer will then need to clean-up this code using clean up methods.

3.11 Global Assembly Cache (GAC)

The GAC is a machine wide code cache that stores assemblies shared by applications running on that computer. Although, a useful feature, only use the GAC when you need to it is because you can easily end up with a string of dependencies that will lead to support problems. The best strategy is probably to keep the assemblies in the same directory structure as the application and only share assemblies in the GAC when you really need to. Keeping assemblies in an application directory does not prevent them from being accessible to unmanaged code or COM interoperability.

If you do need to use the GAC, the GAC tool is a part of the .NET Framework SDK that allows assemblies to be copied into it. Failing that, Windows Explorer can be used to simply drag-and-drop files across. Use of the Windows Explorer is only advisable when running in a development environment since it does not provide assembly reference counting or other management features.

The GAC resides in the WINNT directory, so it will inherit that directory's Access Control List. Therefore, access needs to be limited to trusted administrators only. Any assemblies placed into the GAC will need to be strongly named since they will undergo integrity checks to ensure that they have not been damaged or altered in any way.

3.12 Visual Studio.NET Solution Deployment

A huge issue for developers writing applications prior to Visual Studio.NET has been deployment. Building a server and deploying a solution can be a very daunting prospect, particularly if you need to have subsequent rebuilds, since it is extremely difficult to achieve a clean machine devoid of any old components. This component conflict has been neatly named "DLL hell" since the DLL versions end up causing no end of conflicts and software errors.

Visual Studio.NET has three automated types of deployment:

1. *Merge Module Project, packages components that might be shared by multiple applications.* Components (.msm files) are created that allow setup code to be shared between Windows Installers. A merge module is created that contains all of the resources, registry entries, dependencies, and setup logic needed for that installation.

2.   *Setup Project builds an installer for a Windows-based application.*
The Windows installer file (.msi) has all of the components, files,
registry settings, and instructions for the installation. Two types
of setup projects can be created: one for traditional Windows
applications that installs the files in a specified server directory
and a Web setup project that deploys the solution to a virtual
directory on a Web server.

3.   *Cab Project creates a cabinet (.cab) file containing ActiveX controls to
be downloaded to a Web browser.* Any dependencies need to be
handled manually.

For some applications, the use of Visual Studio deployment tools may
be overkill, so the developer has a couple of more simple ways to deploy
applications:

■   *The Copy Project command is used to deploy a Web-based application.*
Because it does not use the deployment tools, it will only copy files
across onto the target Web server. No configuration settings are carried over, so this is probably better used for subsequent file copies
after initial deployment.

■   *XCOPY is probably the most basic method of copying files across.* It will
use the MSDOS XCOPY command to copy files from one place to
another. No configuration settings are copied, and there is no automatic file protection, which could result in files accidentally being
overwritten.

3.12.1   Visual Studio.NET Technology Decisions

The downside of having so much technology at hand is the need to choose
a suitable combination for a particular solution.

3.13   Web Forms or Windows Forms?

The first choice is whether you need to go the rich client/Windows Forms
route or the browser-based Web Forms solution. Naturally any solution
designed for a Web site will need to be based on Web Forms; also, a solution
that is transaction intense and that must make full use of the Windows API
will need to be written using Windows Forms. In the early days of Microsoft
Internet development tools, the choice was more straightforward since the

Figure 3.8
*When building a
Web form, Visual
Studio
automatically
builds a
corresponding Web
site infrastructure.*

capability of the Web-based environment was very limited. Now both options offer a good range of capabilities, and sometimes the decision is less clear-cut.

Windows Forms are ideal if you are writing an application that includes intensive graphics, data access, or games-type solutions. All of these will rely on the client PC to deliver computing power and resources. Often local PC settings will be needed in such places as the registry and local file system. All of the graphics classes in the Windows GDI+ are available to Windows Forms, making them better positioned for the more intensive applications.

Web Forms are platform independent and therefore better designed for broad-reaching applications that need to be run on different browsers or devices. Deploying a Web Forms application is much easier than a Windows Forms application since there is no client-side code needed—they only need a browser to run. Access to local resources, such as the registry or file system, is not possible since the application will run in the browser context, which automatically prevents direct system access and possible security breaches (see Figure 3.8).

3.14 Windows Service, XML Web Service, or .NET Component?

As well as building "normal" solutions, Visual Studio can be used to build other types of applications that provide services or support to a more mainstream solution.

Windows service applications are essentially long-running Windows executables or applications. They can be started at boot time and managed as a service, but they do not have a user interface; instead they provide a background service often used by other applications. They are useful if you wish to start an application on a user's PC without the user having to invoke the application.

XML Web services are explained in Chapter 9. They provide a loosely coupled architecture that enables services to be accessed from across the Internet and are seen as the preferred way of building distributed solutions. Previously the developer would have considered Distributed COM, or DCOM; but that has limitations when used across the Internet. XML Web services use a set of standard Internet technologies including SOAP, XML, and HTTP.

Building applications from reusable components has been a goal of developers for many years. By building a set of standard chunks of reusable code that has been tested and debugged, applications can be assembled far more quickly than if developers had to write the same functionality over again. .NET components are the updated way of building reusable chunks of code, and a number of development shops are starting to build libraries of components for use across all new developments.

3.15   Web User Controls and Web Custom Controls

If you need to build an application using server-based controls, but none of those provided in ASP.NET are suitable, it is possible to create your own. Web user controls are generally easier to build than custom controls, but are more difficult to use since they cannot be added to the Visual Studio toolbox; instead, they are represented as a default icon or glyph when they are placed on a form. This provides a maintenance problem since the components cannot be shared, and each developer using them needs to have a copy of the control installed locally.

Web custom controls must be written in code, but they can then be added to the toolbox and used like any other control. In addition, the control can be placed in the global assembly cache and shared between applications.

3.16   Server-Based Application Development

Every Visual Studio.NET solution will need to interact with server-based resources such as databases, message queues, and event logs. This has often proven difficult in the past since tying together such disparate resources is anything but easy. The early days of "*n*" tier or multiple-layer applications as espoused in Microsoft's short-lived Windows DNA strategy were pretty tough due to the difficult process of hooking the technologies together.

As discussed earlier, Visual Studio.NET now comes with a Server Explorer, which lists all of the available server resources in one place. Visual Studio 6.0 had the ability to explore SQL Server and Oracle databases, but this has now been extended to cover most resources you are likely to need. By using the Component Designer and the Server Explorer together server-side components can be created using a drag-and-drop approach.

One of the most commonly used server-side resources is Microsoft Message Queue (MSMQ). This allows messages to be sent from one application to another asynchronously, but with a guarantee that the message will arrive even if the network is down and the message needs to be queued for later submission. While not suitable for every business scenario, it does lend itself well to the disconnected nature of the Internet. MSMQ also provides connectivity to IBM MQ Series, which provides messaging functions across the range of IBM platforms, including AS400 and System 390. The MSMQ component in the Visual Studio Server Explorer allows developers to send and receive messages using a couple of lines of code.

The Windows Event Log is an increasingly useful server resource for developers to use. Although initially designed for use by Microsoft Windows as a way of tracking down errors, the Event Log has now been extended and is the place of choice for Visual Studio.Net developers to write relevant event-related messages from within their applications. Customized event logs can be created and managed if this is more appropriate for a specific application. Events can also be set to trigger pager messages or other tasks.

3.17 Schedules, Schedules, Schedules

Like the white rabbit in *Alice in Wonderland* suggests, keeping dates is important, and dropping a schedule can have some pretty bad effects. Most organizations have routine tasks that must be executed hourly, daily, weekly, or monthly. With the increasing demand for immediate business results, a number of large organizations are able to determine their financial position on a daily basis by executing scheduled tasks.

Visual Studio.NET has extended the scheduling capability from earlier versions of Visual Studio so that complex schedules and tasks can be set up. The schedule component is dragged from the toolbox into the Component Designer, and then properties are set to determine when the component wakes and executes a task (see Figure 3.9).

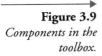

Figure 3.9
Components in the
toolbox.

3.18 Directory Watching and Performance Counters

Similar to BizTalk Server (see Chapter 4), Visual Studio.NET comes with a directory watching component. A directory can be monitored, and as soon as a file appears or changes, an event can be fired by the monitoring component.

Performance counters are an important way of measuring how an application is coping under pressure. This has been a feature of Windows NT and Windows 2000 for awhile, and Visual Studio.NET has a performance counter component that enables Visual Studio to read a specific performance parameter or to write to a performance counter. This can be used during an application design phase or as an ongoing measure of performance, maybe raising an event to the Event Log if a bottleneck is in danger of appearing.

4

Microsoft BizTalk Server

Almost every organization has a requirement to access and share information. The chances are that if you thought through the types of data and systems in your organization, the list would soon start to grow. Typically, this would cover spreadsheets, small databases, organization, relational databases, and mainframe-hosted systems.

Tying these systems together is a complex process, often named Enterprise Application Integration (EAI). One standard approach to EAI has been to implement tactical solutions, linking system A to system B, system C to system D, and so on, resulting in a whole serious of point-to-point connections. Each time a link is added, the EAI team will need to put in a series of services, such as message management, transaction management, and recovery services, that entail even more work. The end result can best be described as a cat's cradle of connections (see Figure 4.1).

Figure 4.1
A typical connection scenario.

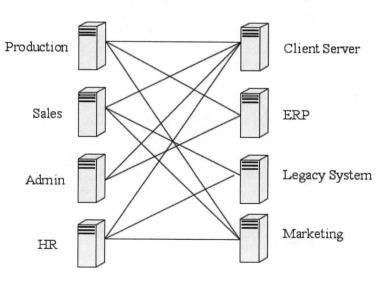

Production   Client Server

Sales   ERP

Admin   Legacy System

HR   Marketing

Microsoft BizTalk Server is one of the Microsoft .NET Enterprise Server products designed to provide a central messaging hub, which, combined with business process management, makes EAI a more achievable goal. In addition to its inward looking EAI role, BizTalk Server also provides a messaging system capable of receiving, translating, and then retransmitting documents in a manner similar to conventional Electronic Data Interchange, or EDI.

4.1   A Brief History of EDI

EDI has been in use since the mid-1960s, when a group of railroad companies formed an organization to improve the quality of transportation data being transferred from company to company. Retail companies also saw the opportunity to use EDI as a way of integrating with their suppliers and started an initiative to build industry-specific EDI solutions. Over the years other standards started to emerge, and in 1985 EDIFACT (EDI for Administration, Commerce, and Transport) was created through the United Nations.

4.1.1   EDI and BizTalk Server

Although there are some similarities between EDI and BizTalk Server, there are also some notable areas in which the approaches differ.

EDI has gained widespread acceptance and, since the standard has been established for a number of years, many large organizations use EDI as an intrinsic part of their everyday business. There are limitations with EDI, notably the cost of setup, and maintenance can be high as can the use of the value added networks (VANS) necessary to "hook" into EDI systems. In addition, EDI is a useful tool for server-based connections outside of a business, but would not be used as an organization's enterprise application integration platform (see Figure 4.2).

BizTalk Server supports EDI formats and receipting, which is sufficient for interoperating with many EDI-based systems. BizTalk Server does not currently provide a fully fledged EDI-based environment and therefore does have a number of limitations for those wishing to undertake a full EDI-based implementation with the product. A number of these limitations can be overcome using customized code within BizTalk Server, but that is additional functionality that an organization would need to purchase separately.

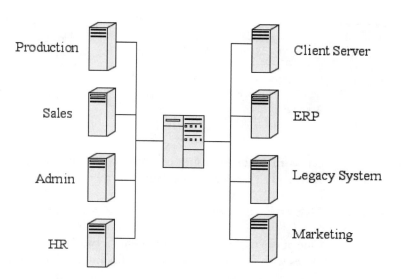

Figure 4.2
Hub-and-spoke EAI.

As I guess you would expect by now the interchange of data uses XML with the messages containing self-describing data. This message can be unravelled by BizTalk Server, and, if necessary, appropriate business processes can be executed on receipt of the message. In addition, BizTalk Server comes with a set of tools that enables the XML message to be converted into a number of other document formats, including EDI850, UN/EDIFACT, and comma separated values (CSV), providing the important integration hooks (see Figure 4.3).

4.1.2   BizTalk Server and Web Services

It is important to understand the differences between Web services and BizTalk Server functionality because they can be confusing. In essence, as we can see in Figure 4.4, BizTalk is a useful mechanism for transferring business documents and integrating with existing ERP-type systems. Web services, on the other hand, are a way of exposing application functionality

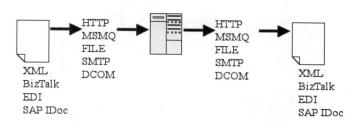

Figure 4.3
BizTalk Server supports a number of different file formats and submission routes.

Figure 4.4
*Comparing Web
services and
BizTalk Server.*

across the Internet using common protocols such as SOAP and HTTP/
XML. Web services are explained further in Chapter 9.

4.1.3   BizTalk Server Messaging Services

One of the useful features of BizTalk Server is that the application that integrates with BizTalk Server never really knows that BizTalk Server is actually
there. All the source application or system needs to do is produce a file containing the data, which is then picked up by BizTalk Server. This could be
as simple as placing a file into an appropriate network directory. This is

Figure 4.5
*Setting up Receive
function properties
for an advanced
shipping notice.*

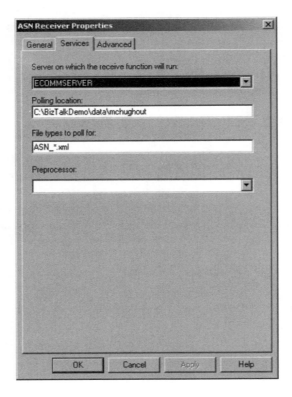

heart warming to many EAI practitioners because the interface is noninvasive—that is, you don't have to mess around with the internals of the source application since most systems are capable of providing simple data extracts on a regular basis. Failing that, there is a screen scraping option but that is functionality outside of the scope of BizTalk Server and something you will need to implement yourself using the appropriate software tools.

The file submission need not be in real time. BizTalk Server is just as happy to work asynchronously and pick up files based on a specific time rather than as soon as they appear. Again, this will be dictated by the business model you are working with. This also gives some protection from network failure since after a network outage, BizTalk Server will revisit appropriate directories and pick up any outstanding files.

To configure a document pickup, the BizTalk Server administrators use the Receive functions in the BizTalk Server administration tool. The dialog allows you to set the server and polling location details (see Figure 4.5).

The Advanced tab allows the document destination to be set up. As well as picking up files from a directory, BizTalk Server allows files to be submitted via HTTP, message queuing, SMTP, and COM from within an application.

The file destination is called a message port in BizTalk Server, and here you can set up where the file goes; if the file is to go to multiple destinations; you can setup distribution lists (see Figure 4.6).

BizTalk Server also supports the use of channels. A channel determines what happens to a file before it reaches its final destination. Typically a file will need to be manipulated, transformed, or signed at some point on its journey, and this is what the channel is designed to do (see Figure 4.7).

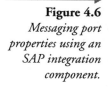

Figure 4.6
Messaging port properties using an SAP integration component.

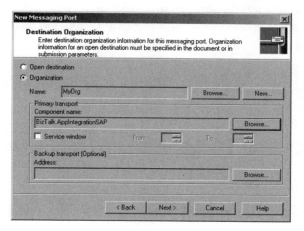

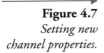

Figure 4.7
Setting new channel properties.

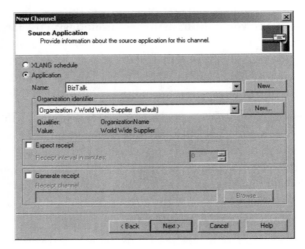

4.1.4   Document Definitions and the BizTalk Editor

Given the choice of using Notepad or a decent tool to create XML documents, most people would choose a decent tool. Luckily, BizTalk Server comes with such a beast called the BizTalk Editor. This tool is designed to reduce the chore of writing XML script and, hopefully, the number of errors that are bound to creep into any heavy manual authoring process (see Figure 4.8).

The BizTalk Editor can be used to display and edit any BizTalk Server–supported document format, including EDI or CSV files. Once a specifica-

Figure 4.8
The BizTalk Editor.

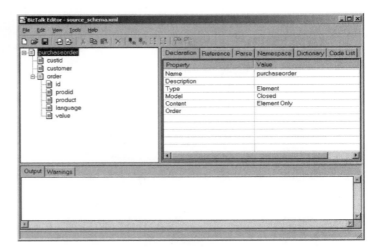

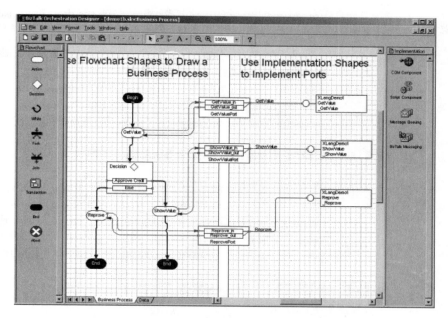

tion has been set up, it is saved to the WebDAV repository. WebDAV is the World Wide Web Document Authoring and Versioning standard designed to support collaborative authoring across the World Wide Web. It is an open standard maintained by the Internet Engineering Task Force, or IETF. The document definition is the specification you built in the BizTalk Editor combined with a name given to it within BizTalk Server. With this approach you can have multiple document definitions, all based on the same specification.

4.1.5 Business Process Orchestration

Once the document definitions and channels have been configured, you need to be able to define what happens to the files when they are received by BizTalk Server. In BizTalk Server, this is known as business process orchestration. Based on Microsoft Visio, the BizTalk Server orchestration tool allows a nontechnical business expert to define what happens to the file graphically by drawing the images on the screen. All of the traditional business flow chart tools are available, so that actions, decisions, whiles, and transactions can be modeled graphically and in a fairly easy-to-use way. Multiple activities can be tied up into single transactions if failure of any one component must lead to a rollback of a piece of work, similar to a database transaction (see Figure 4.9). The business expert can then hand the process workflow over to a developer, who is then responsible for translating the workflow into a technical equivalent.

A lot of the coding work has been removed since the developer can use a set of predefined components and drag-and-drop them onto the developer side of the screen. The three fundamental shapes are the COM component, message queuing, and BizTalk messaging shapes, and these will probably form the basis for most systems a developer will design.

4.1.6 COM Component Shape

This allows BizTalk Server to work with other preexisting COM components or other applications. When this shape is used, the COM component binding wizard is invoked and a set of questions is run through. If you are using COM+ components, you will be presented with additional questions associated with the transaction support required for your component.

4.1.7 Message Queuing Shape

This allows an XLANG schedule to communicate with another XLANG schedule or application by placing messages into a queue, which is then read. Using the message queue shape will invoke the message queuing binding wizard, which will take the developer through the steps of configuring how the queue will be used. If the nature of the queue is likely to change, then a dynamic queue can be configured, or alternatively, if the queue is unlikely to change, then a static queue is set up. Messages can also be filtered to ensure that they contain sender information, if required, prior to being submitted to the queue.

4.1.8 BizTalk Messaging Shape

This is the BizTalk messaging services shape used to configure message exchange between BizTalk orchestration services and the messaging engine. When used, the BizTalk messaging binding wizard appears, taking you through the configuration settings required. This includes the communication direction, which tells BizTalk Server if it is sending or receiving documents, and channel information about where to place the documents.

Other tasks can be custom built as script components using any of the standard scripting tools, such as VBScript, but the chances are that you will (and maybe should!) use the COM component for most of the external connections you make.

Figure 4.10
*BizTalk server
components.*

To join the two sides of the diagram together a line is drawn in a typical Visio way that hooks the analyst's view into the implementation view. The BizTalk Server communication wizard will then prompt for some extra details on how the shapes will talk to each other. Finally, the data page is completed; this determines how the business document will flow from one process to another.

The business process orchestration drawing is formally known as the XLANG drawing, and the drawing plus developer implementation is the XLANG schedule. The schedule is written to a file in the XLANG language, which uses XML to represent the business process and technological implementation. To convert the diagram into the final XLANG language representation there is an option under the file menu called "make XLANG filename.skx," which does this for you. BizTalk Server components are shown in Figure 4.10.

4.1.9 The BizTalk Mapper

BizTalk Mapper is the tool used to transform an XML document from one schema to another. It uses standard XSL Transformations (XSLT), which is a W3C-approved language for transforming XML schemata. The tool pro-

Figure 4.11
*Biztalk Mapper
with three
functoids to assist
the
transformations.*

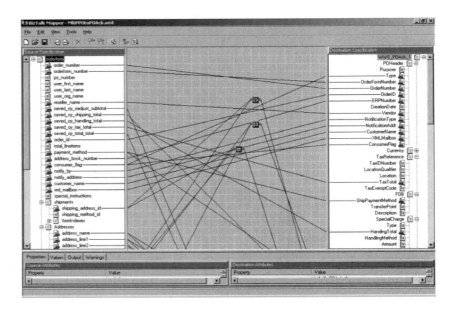

vides a neat interface on top of this language, so all a developer needs to do is drag-and-drop links from one schema to another.

If this simple one-to-one relationship is not enough, BizTalk Mapper comes with functoids. These delightfully named transformation elements allow all sorts of processing to happen as part of the transformation process, such as string manipulation, mathematical functions, and scientific operations. These are very similar to Microsoft Excel functions, and the BizTalk Mapper ships with 60 or so of these in the box. If you want a customized function, there is a script functoid, which allows you to write custom code in VBScript. Functoids can be linked or cascaded, so that results from one can be passed to another (see Figure 4.11).

4.1.10   BizTalk Server and Protocols

As already discussed, BizTalk Server supports a number of protocols that allow it to receive and transmit documents between organizations. Deciding which protocol to use will depend on a number of factors. For example, what protocols does your partner organization support? Are you using a private network or the Internet? How secure does the transmission need to be? And so on. Probably the most popular protocol will be HTTP or its secure equivalent, HTTPS, simply because these are available to all across the Internet.

Probably the most straightforward way of receiving HTTP inbound messages is to use an ASP script, which accepts the incoming document and then sets it to one side in a file directory, ready for collection by Biz-Talk Server.

Using this asynchronous approach, the document sender is simply sent an acknowledgment that the document has arrived safely, whether or not BizTalk Server has subsequently picked up the message for processing. Although this may appear fragile, it is more than suitable for many business scenarios since BizTalk Server will pick up and process the message in what I tend to call "real-enough time" rather than real time.

Forcing BizTalk Server to operate in a real-time mode by submitting the documents directly via the COM interface is fine, but you will need to accept that should the system fail, the document originator will not receive an acknowledgment when he or she submits the document, and the system would be seen to have failed. Again, the business needs to decide which scenario best fits its objectives.

To improve on this directory/temporary storage–based document submission, BizTalk Server comes ready to use Microsoft Message Queue (MSMQ). Instead of the document being parked in a directory location, it will be posted to a message queue and then posted to BizTalk Server using a message queue Receive function.

4.1.11   Application Integration Components (AIC)

Since the release of BizTalk Server, there have been a large number of third parties that have built AICs to connect BizTalk Server with a large range of back-end business systems. The AIC allows the exchange of documents between BizTalk Server and the business system, managing transport, security, and serialization where appropriate.

The AICs are COM objects that BizTalk Server will call when delivering data to the back-end system. Assuming that the message port is configured to call the AIC, each time BizTalk Server needs to send a document, the component is automatically instantiated and the data passed back. The AIC is responsible for all of the underlying communication to the back-end system, using whatever API calls or database access it needs.

There are two models for building AICs:

1.   *Pipeline components are used when the component requires configuration properties.* These components have been included to support integration between BizTalk Server and Commerce Server/

Figure 4.12
*MQSeries and
BizTalk Server
architecture.*

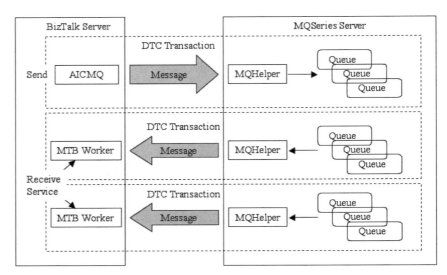

Site Server. Pipeline components written for the Commerce Server commerce interchange pipeline are, therefore, compatible with BizTalk Server components written this way.

2. *Lightweight components use a far simpler interface, which is much easier to build than pipeline components.* By default BizTalk Server will query the component to see if the lightweight model is being used, and if it is not, it will then query for pipeline interfaces.

Once built the AICs need to be registered so that BizTalk Server understands where the components are and how they can be used. The AIC can be registered as either an in-process or out-of-process component. In-process delivers better performance, but if the component should fail, then Biz-Talk Server will probably terminate, so the usual out-of-process registration is normally used.

4.1.12   SAP and MQSeries Integration with BizTalk Server

Integrating BizTalk Server with existing line of business systems is an important consideration for many users of BizTalk Server and application integration components; many line of business solutions can be obtained from third parties.

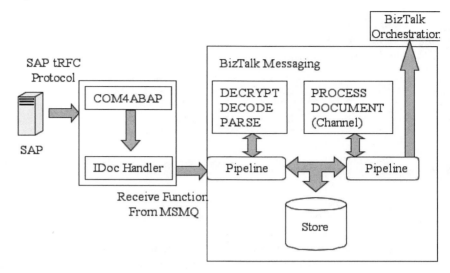

Figure 4.13
Receiving an IDoc from SAP.

4.1.13 MQSeries

The objective of the Microsoft MQSeries adapter is to allow BizTalk to send and receive messages to MQSeries, particularly when running on non-Windows platforms. The adapter has been designed to be easy to deploy and to support the transactional delivery of all messages. Any messages sent to the MQSeries adapter are guaranteed to be delivered, will only be delivered once, and can be converted from UNICODE to ANSI.

The Receive function for MQSeries runs as a BizTalk Server service and supports up to 100MB of messages at any one time. Distributed transactions are supported, and multiple MQSeries queue managers can be accessed at any one time. An MQHelper is needed if you wish to support distributed transactions, and this will run under dllhost.exe on the MQSeries server (see Figure 4.12).

4.1.14 SAP

The SAP adapter provided by Microsoft is designed to offer a simple solution to integrate BizTalk with SAP. It can be configured in a short time and does not need any software to be installed on the SAP system. The adapter is designed to allow BizTalk Server to send and receive SAP IDocs and will support any SAP IDoc format (see Figures 4.13 and 4.14).

The adapter supports XML schema generation and allows the SAP Business Objects Repository (BOR) to be accessed via Remote Function Calls

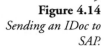

Figure 4.14
Sending an IDoc to SAP.

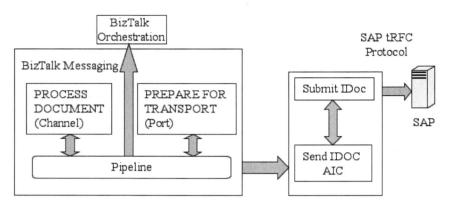

(RFCs). The IDoc structures are retrieved from the BOR and converted to document specifications. Multiple SAP systems can be sorted from one BizTalk Server, and the IDoc delivery is guaranteed since the adapter uses the Distributed Transaction Coordinator between com4abap, SQL Server, and MSMQ to deliver documents.

Setting up the SAP adapter is reasonably straightforward. Accounts need to be set up for com4abap and the adapter to access SAP. RFC ports are then configured, and document destinations, customer profiles, and SAP business processes are also configured.

Figure 4.15 *Hub-based BizTalk Server for small and medium-sized organizations.*

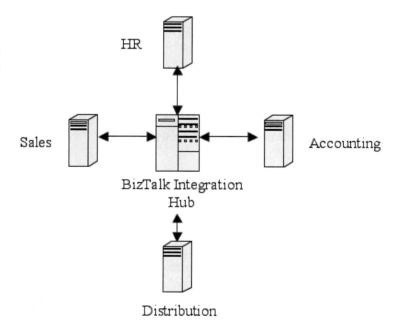

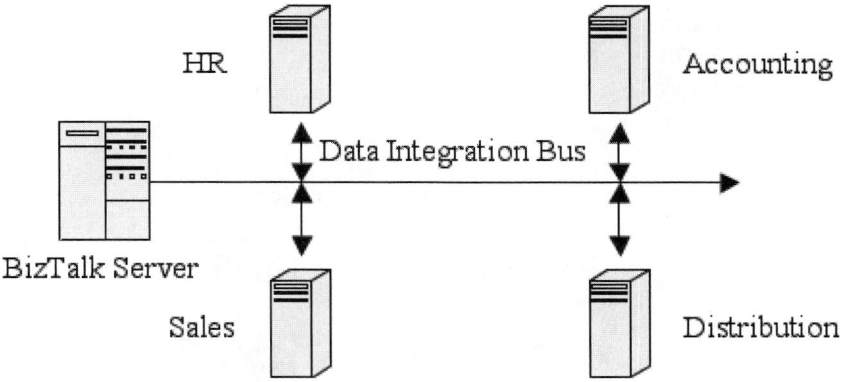

Figure 4.16
*Using BizTalk
Server as a data
bus.*

4.2   BizTalk Server Deployment

Deploying a BizTalk Server configuration can be an involved process, depending upon the business requirements.

Small and medium-sized organizations can often use a single BizTalk Server as a routing and transformation hub. All of the necessary channels, schedules, and ports are built to support the specific integration requirements (see Figure 4.15).

Larger organizations should probably consider the use of a more distributed and manageable solution than the single small-business hub. This distributed architecture is often referred to as publish and subscribe, shortened to Pub-Sub, and it allows an element of abstraction so that publishers and subscribers to data is unaware of each other. With this model, systems can be plugged and unplugged from the data integration bus with no impact on any other publisher or subscriber. BizTalk Server can be configured to support this data bus approach (see Figure 4.16).

Whatever architecture is chosen, typical deployment considerations would include the following:

- Security and firewalls
- Scalability and load balancing
- The design of the BizTalk Server groups
- Setup of messaging and orchestration services

Figure 4.17
*Secure BizTalk
configuration for
Web access.*

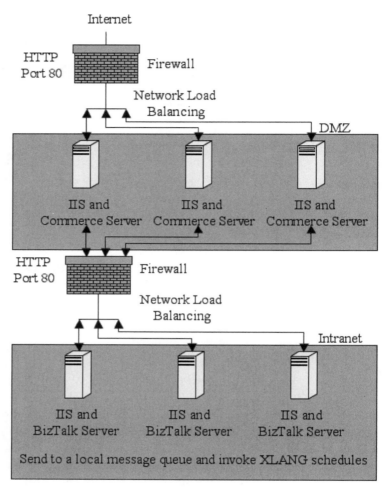

4.2.1 Security and Firewalls

Of importance to any integrated system permitting files to be submitted from "foreign" sources is security. Most of BizTalk Server security is based on either Windows 2000 or Microsoft SQL Server, which is used to keep data secure in the messaging management database. If you are building COM+ components, either SQL Server or Windows authentication can be used.

Windows 2000 security features, and therefore BizTalk Server, include the following:

- Public-key infrastructure
- Microsoft component services
- Microsoft Cryptography API
- Kerberos Protocol

Certificates are a useful tool for securing data with a trading partner, but do require some time-consuming management and, for large-scale installations, may prove to be a significant administration overhead. Probably a more popular model would be to use Secure Sockets Layer, or SSL. SSL is a feature of Internet Information Server, IIS, that negotiates an encryption algorithm between a Web client and server, checks key information, and authenticates the validity of the server to the client. Data is then encrypted using session keys negotiated in the initial handshake process.

Most organizations would use a firewall to restrict network traffic to HTTPS and FTP protocols. A limited number of other ports may be opened, such as port 80 for HTTP, and double firewalls are often put in place to isolate Web servers from an internal LAN (see Figure 4.17).

4.2.2 Scalability and Load Balancing

There are three layers to BizTalk Server: the BizTalk services, SQL Server, and the transport services. All of these can influence how any BizTalk Server installation will perform at any time. BizTalk Server supports either scaling up or scaling out, depending upon the strategy that you wish to adopt (see Chapter 10 for further details).

To scale up a BizTalk Server installation, all of the usual rules apply—fast processor with a large level III cache, SMP box with eight processors, 512MB RAM, multiple disks and controllers for message queuing, distributed transaction coordinator, and dual network cards. In addition, BizTalk Server ideally needs to run on a dedicated server to ensure full access to these resources.

4.2.3 HTTP/HTTPS

If you are using HTTP/HTTPS, configure the inbound Receive service on a server separate from BizTalk Server. If you must use the same server, add additional hardware to cater to the processing of inbound documents. Some organizations I have worked with have failed to cater to this inbound traffic, which has significantly affected BizTalk Server performance.

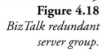

Figure 4.18
BizTalk redundant server group.

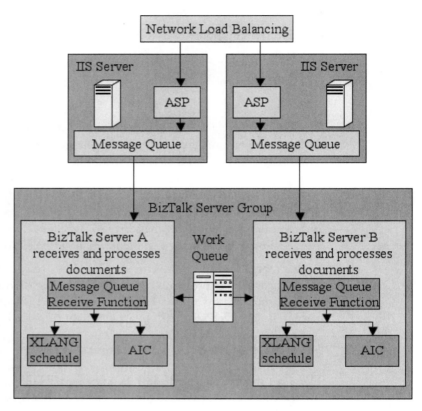

4.2.4 File Receive

The file Receive function can be sped up by placing the receive directory on a local server rather than a network server. This removes the network latency; although small per file received, it can soon mount up. Using a disk array can also improve throughput.

4.2.5 SMTP

SMTP is designed for network e-mail, and as such is not as scalable as it could be when used to deliver documents to BizTalk Server. Any SMTP product—be it Microsoft Exchange or another—will need to have additional hardware added to ensure it is able to cope with BizTalk Server document submission. If you plan to use S/MIME, expect even further degradation in performance unless you add significant additional hardware.

4.2.6 **Message Queuing**

Transactional, local queues on BizTalk Server are much preferred to remote queues; they avoid network latency and the need to query Active Directory. Extra performance can be gained by switching off transactional queues, but nontransactional queues will not offer the same level of reliability.

4.3   **Designing BizTalk Server Groups**

A BizTalk Server group is a collection of centrally managed individual Biz-Talk Servers that need to be monitored and configured together. BizTalk uses a number of queues to process incoming and outgoing documents, and a BizTalk Server group can contain servers doing all of these tasks or allocate a specific role to individual servers within the group to achieve better performance and fault tolerance.

The redundant server group configuration has all of the group BizTalk Servers configured to share the same queue, tracking, and messaging database. In this case an ASP page is created to receive incoming documents and place them into the appropriate message queue, which is then placed into the work queue. Whichever server is available will then pick up the document from the queue and process it, allowing any server in the group to process incoming documents (see Figure 4.18).

In the partitioned or specialized server group, the BizTalk Servers are configured to share the same queue, tracking, and messaging management database, but at least one server is configured to receive documents from the HTTP transport service. When a document arrives in the message queue, it is picked up and submitted to another BizTalk Server. The end result is faster processing of documents since they are prevented from building up in the message queue (see Figure 4.19).

4.3.1 **BizTalk 2002 Developments**

BizTalk 2002 introduced a number of new features to the product:

- Deployment of BizTalk solutions has been difficult, because there were limited tools to assist in the development/staging/deployment cycle. BizTalk 2002 introduced a set of drivers that allows it to work with Application Center Server (see Chapter 8), improving the deployment across multiple servers.

Figure 4.19
*BizTalk
partitioned or
specialized server
group.*

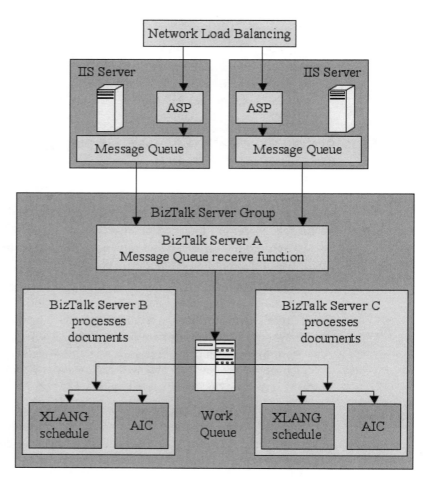

- Super Effective and Efficient Delivery, or SEED was developed by the internal IT group at Microsoft. The idea was to reduce the amount of time and effort it took to connect a BizTalk Server to multiple trading partners. SEED gives trading partners a user interface to configure and test their BizTalk connections.

- A set of new monitoring tools designed for use with Microsoft Operations Manager, or MOM contains 900 preset alerts and rules for use in customizing a BizTalk installation.

- The BizTalk Server Toolkit for Microsoft .NET, which now comes with BizTalk Server, allows business process orchestration with XML Web services. In addition, orchestration has been improved, allowing separate transaction and exception handling, XLANG schedule pooling, and XLANG correlation, which allows multiple schedule instances to use a single message queue.

- A new HTTP Receive function is now included, configured from within BizTalk Server and designed to give fast performance.

- Database management and utilities have been improved, allowing the SQL Server database used by BizTalk Server to be managed directly. This provides useful features, such as manual restore of databases, deletion of records from the persistence database, and automatic expiration of timed-out items in the tracking database.

- The BizTalk Server administration console can now be installed on a remote computer and allowed to manage any BizTalk Server in that environment.

- SQL Server integrated security, which now allows BizTalk Server to use Windows 2000 credentials to determine privileges rather than SQL Server credentials.

Microsoft Commerce Server

Commerce Server is designed for use by organizations that wish to sell products or services across the Internet. It evolved from the first Microsoft business-to-consumer products called Site Server and Site Server Commerce Edition.

Since these early days, Commerce Server has taken the best features of these original products and updated them to provide a fairly comprehensive product for building, deploying, and managing Web sites to sell goods or services to users (see Figure 5.1).

Figure 5.1
Typical Commerce Server–based Web site.

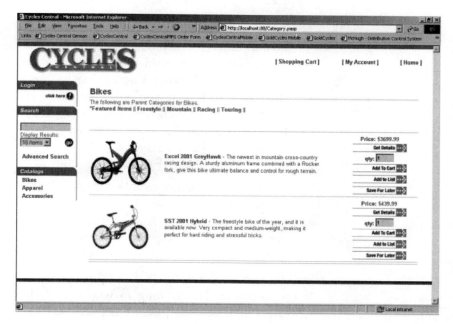

Figure 5.2
Commerce Server pipeline.

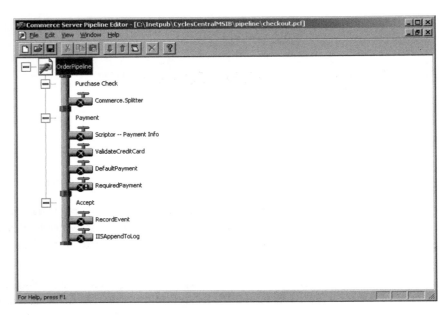

Commerce Server comprises five main elements, each of which can be customized or adapted by Commerce Server developers:

1. *Product catalogs.* The product catalog system is the heart of Commerce Server and is used to store the products and services that are sold on the Web site. Catalogs can be imported or exported in XML or CSV format, and the catalog supports a range of searching capabilities, such as freetext, property, and specification searches. Catalog data can be exchanged between Commerce Servers using BizTalk Server.

2. *Profiles.* The profiling system in Commerce Server enables organizations or individuals to be profiled and relevant data collected about those visiting your site. Catalog-based information can be customized to suit specific profiles, so, for example, visitors from certain companies are presented with a tailored catalog with goods and pricing to match a prenegotiated deal.

3. *Business analytics.* Any active Web site is likely to collect huge amounts of data relating to who visited the Web site, which pages they looked at, what was purchased, and so on. The activity logs from Commerce Server can be exported to Microsoft

Figure 5.3
Setting pipeline component properties.

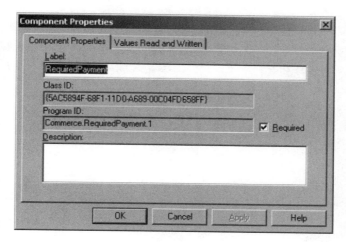

SQL Server OLAP services and then data mined in a data warehouse OLAP cube.

4.   *Commerce Server pipelines.* The business process flow is built using Commerce Server pipelines, which take an order through the purchase cycle and start to link in other business processes as needed to satisfy an order (see Figures 5.2 and 5.3).

5.   *Targeting system.* Targeting individuals or groups of users is one of the clever ways of increasing sales. By working out who a user is and his or her particular interests, the targeting system can then intelligently propose up-sell or cross-sell opportunities to site visitors. With the predictive algorithms created by Microsoft Research and now incorporated into Commerce Server, buying patterns can be estimated and very specific offers made.

Figure 5.4 illustrates the Commerce Server architecture.

5.1   **The Commerce Server Manager**

This is the Windows 2000 Microsoft Management Console (MMC) application that manages Commerce Server resources, sites, applications, and Web Servers.

A Commerce Server resource provides functionality to applications in a Commerce Server site. Normally consisting of COM components, which

Figure 5.4
Commerce Server
architecture.

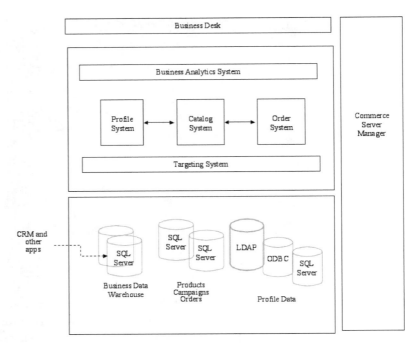

are controlled from the application Web pages, resource properties are stored in the Commerce Server administration database (see Figure 5.5).

Resources can be global or site specific. Global resources include the direct mailer engine used to send personalized e-mail to users, predictor service to identify usage trends, the data warehouse, authentication and identification services, and profiles. Site-specific resources are relevant only to a specific site you are running and include application configuration data, such as billing and payment information, campaign configurations, the product catalog, shopping-basket transactions, and shipping/tax data.

Most Commerce Server sites have both a user site for visitors to make purchases and a business desk or administration site to control business-related functions. Both of these sites use the Commerce Server object model and ASP pages to modify resources such as the administration database.

5.2   The Business Desk

Business managers will spend their time managing a Commerce Server site using the business desk application. This can range from changing price

Figure 5.5
Commerce Server Manager.

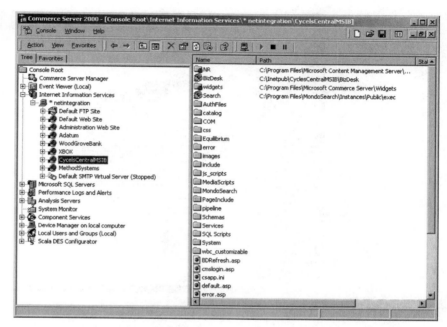

information to running activity reports against the activity logs (see Figure 5.6).

The business desk has two elements. The business desk application is used to manage and analyze a site and is available via a secure login to support remote access. The business desk client is software that is installed on a local client that will then connect to the business desk application. There are possible performance implications when using the client to access the business desk, and Microsoft recommends that a high-speed line be installed between the client and the business desk. This is not suitable for use across a slow-speed hotel connection!

The business desk does use role-based security, so that only users with appropriate rights can manage specific modules. Any user not permitted to use a piece of business desk functionality will automatically have that module removed from his or her navigation window within the business desk. While this will not prevent a targeted attack on your site from within the business desk, it does prevent users from working on modules that are not in their remit. In addition, this level of security does not prevent the data being changed directly in the SQL Server database used to store the site information. If you need this additional security, the database will have to be secured using SQL Server features.

Figure 5.6 *The business desk.*

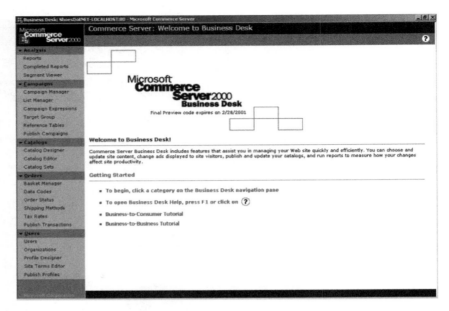

5.3   Commerce Server Campaigns

Campaigns are the bread-and-butter tool of marketing people using your site. By combining the data from the data warehouse and profile-based information, it is possible to put in place some well-targeted activities.

Commerce Server campaigns would typically cover a number of areas, including the following:

- Discounts on specific items
- Direct mail sent to a user's e-mail address
- Embedded advertisement on relevant site pages

By using the Commerce Server Content Selection Framework (CSF) site, content can be modularized so that specific content or advertisement is placed on relevant pages. This can also include displaying products to exploit cross-sell or up-sell opportunities.

Specific advertisement can be created with a number of attributes familiar to marketing professionals, including tools to prevent conflicting ads from appearing on the same page and need of delivery (NOD), which

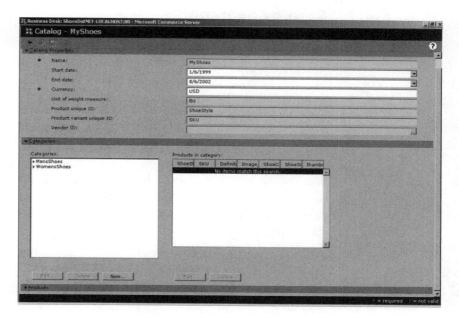

determines how many more ads are remaining from a block advertisement purchase.

5.4 The Product Catalog

Products or services that are being sold on your site are all stored in the product catalog. The catalog will normally reside on a Microsoft SQL Server and in practice will build a fairly complex database structure with something like 120 tables (see Figure 5.7)!

The basic catalog will contain categories and products, but no specific pricing rules, only the base product prices. Commerce Server allows you to build custom catalogs that are derived from base catalogs on a site. Prices in the custom catalog override those given in the base catalog and are used to offer special pricing deals to particular partners or customers. They are also useful in a traditional retail site since product pricing can be adapted based, for example, on the membership level of a site visitor.

Catalog sets are used to determine which catalog a user will see when visiting a site. A catalog set is a group of one or more catalogs that can be displayed to specific users or organizations.

5.4.1   Catalog Searching

The catalog can be searched in three ways:

1.   Free text

2.   Query based

3.   Specification

Free text allows you to search catalogs using words or phrases. In practice, this uses the free-text search engine within Microsoft SQL Server since the catalogs reside there. With a SQL Server free-text search, a broader range of search predicates can be used, such as CONTAINS and FREETEXT, above and beyond the typical SQL WHERE clause.

Query searches are similar to free-text searches, but you do not have the benefit of full-text indexing.

Specification searches are a way of iteratively refining a search until the final results are obtained. A good example would be searching for a laptop PC, where you would specify the amount of RAM you needed, then the size of hard disk, and then, if it were important to you, the color of the carry bag!

5.4.2   Commerce Server Security

By their very nature most Commerce Server installations will be available on the Internet for anyone to browse and purchase products. Unfortunately, there is a minority of people who will treat this as an opportunity to probe your site and see how secure it is. To counter this, Commerce Server comes with a number of tools and options to help secure the site from attack.

Secure Sockets Layer (SSL) is generally accepted as one of the best security practices for protecting sensitive pages on your site. Typically any page that collects or serves financial data, such as credit-card information, needs to be managed through SSL. This is configured through Internet Information Server (IIS) and through the purchase of a server certificate.

The site itself will need to be locked down with full control on all services, pages, and applications via Access Control Lists (ACL) on an NTFS-based system. In addition, site visitors, or certainly those doing more than initial browsing, will need to be authenticated. The site will need to be protected via firewalls, and depending on the budget available, this may be a one-, two-, or three-firewall solution. Single firewall solutions are easier to manage, but only provide a single hurdle to climb; a three-firewall solution can be extremely expensive, so a compromise two-firewall solution is normally chosen.

Commerce Server supports up to seven authentication modes, four of which are provided by IIS (anonymous, basic, integrated, and certificates) and three that it provides itself (Windows authentication, custom authentication, and autocookie). These are as follows:

- *Windows authentication.* The user login and password are checked against Active Directory or the Security Access Manager (SAM). Access control with Windows authentication can be down to individual site pages and directories.

- *Custom authentication.* Login credentials are checked against a database (normally SQL Server). Login access is required for every page and directory on the site.

- *Autocookie.* Cookies can automatically be generated for guest users so that you can track which areas of your site they are visiting. It is possible to use autocookie and either Windows authentication or custom authentication together in a mixed mode, so that profile data can be gathered about site visitors.

5.5 SQL Server and Commerce Server

Commerce Server is tightly coupled with SQL Server since it uses the latter as a repository for data ranging from user login details to catalog and campaign information. If your organization is thinking about using Commerce Server, you will need to understand SQL Server's database requirements.

5.6 Building a Commerce Server Site

Theoretically, you can build a Commerce Server installation on a single machine, running all of the Commerce Server components, Windows 2000, and SQL Server together. In fact, this book is being written on just such a beast, but there is no way that this could be used in a production environment. The recommended configuration for a small site is a minimum of four servers—two of which are identical machines used to serve the Web pages and the other two of which are SQL Servers running in a server cluster. In this configuration we would also use network load balancing (NLB) to ensure higher availability and two firewalls for security.

Microsoft recommends two four-processor 500MHz servers with 2GB RAM for the SQL Servers in a small configuration. Large configurations are defined as those utilising between 10 and 100 servers, and in this scenario you would have multiple clusters of SQL Server databases. Commerce Server supports both SQL Server 7.0 (with SP2 or later) and 2000, so if you have not upgraded to 2000 yet, you can still use Commerce Server.

5.6.1   Clustering SQL Server and Commerce Server 2000

Active/active clustering enables you to have two SQL Servers up and running (on separate servers), both working on their own unique data sets (known as *shared nothing*). In a Commerce Server environment you could structure the site so that the product catalog runs on one server and the data warehouse runs on the other—thereby getting day-to-day value from the second server investment. The possible downside is that, should a server fail, it will failover to the second server, imposing its workload onto a single server. Would your Web site still work if all of the database workload were running on one server? The other option is an active/passive installation that has a fully redundant second server that is only used on failure of the first server. The upside is that if the machines are the same specification, your postfailure transactional throughput should be the same as before the failure. This is a compromise decision that you need to take, depending on budget, but the splitting of data warehouse and product catalog/commerce features may be a logical structure.

5.7   Commerce Server Data Warehouse and Business Desk Analytics

One thing you won't be short of on your Web site, unless you have no visitors, is data. Commerce Server can collect no end of data from the moment users visit your site to the moment they move on. The Commerce Server data warehouse can import, transform, and manipulate the data, and then have these data presented to business users via the business desk.

The data warehouse can implement the following activites:

- Import Web log files, user profiles, transactions, campaigns, and catalog data from a Web site (Since the data warehouse is based on SQL

Server, these tasks are completed using the data transformation services (DTS) tool.)

- Prepare the data for analysis by populating the data warehouse (OLAP) cubes

- Resolve Internet Protocol (IP) addresses to convert the addresses to readable domain names

- Delete imported log file, test, or archived data to reduce the amount of storage space required within the SQL Server database

The business desk contains a number of modules that allow a business user to analyze site activity. There are a range of reports available out of the box, but others can quite easily be created.

Dynamic reports are those that are generated at run time, so that the most recent data in the data warehouse are used to populate the report. The data that are displayed are not actually stored. Static reports are run immediately, but the data is stored so that the results can be viewed later without rerunning the report.

5.7.1 Segmentation

This is a neat technology that allows analysis of a group of users having similar profile properties and site behaviors. Typically, they would have similar attributes, such as gender, age, or time they visit the site. Once a group of users has been identified, they can be actively targeted with some very focused offers or marketing activities.

5.7.2 Prediction

Once data have been collected in the data warehouse, these data can form the basis of a prediction model. This enables you to see which customers are buying which products and then start to predict trends and possible patterns in future customer activity.

The basis of this is the prediction model, which uses data that have already established a pattern to number crunch raw data using some very complex and peculiar algorithms. The end result is a prediction assessment of a certain behavior from customers analyzed by the model.

A useful implementation of this technology is to suggest to purchasers of a particular product that they may wish to purchase another—a typical cross-sell activity. A good example is a customer buying a gasoline lawn-mower from your site that suggesting to this customer might also purchase some engine lubricating oil.

5.7.3 Payments and Commerce Server

Commerce Server does not ship with a mechanism to check credit cards or authorize payments for goods. Instead, it has a default payment component that can act as a temporary holding place for credit-card details so that applications can be tested. If you wish to fully enable a payment mechanism, you need to purchase a third-party add-in solution. But before doing that, it might be a good idea to understand the typical Web site payment processes available to you (see Figure 5.8).

- *Internet real-time payment allows a user to submit credit-card details, which are then transmitted to a payment service provider, who, in turn, passes the details on to the bank holding the appropriate merchant account.* The bank will check the credit limit on the card and that the billing address matches the one in the bank's records. The advantages of this system are that it is real-time, straightforward to implement, and relatively low-cost. The disadvantages are that a lost connection to the bank will result in lost sales since cards cannot be authorized, and the system can slow down dramatically at times of peak demand.

- *Real-time with batched payment in-house systems are deployed internally to process payments, removing the need for the customer to wait for authorization.* The credit-card details are batched together and then sent across to a bank in one go. The customer receives a message saying his or her order is being processed, and if there is a later authorization problem, the customer is contacted via e-mail (see Figure 5.9).

- *Redirection services are used by some organizations.* As the user pays for the products, her or she is redirected to another site that captures the payment information. The level of payment transparency available to the user does vary, and in many cases the customer is redirected wholly to another Web site, leading to a rather poor experience. The benefit is a much lower transaction cost since these redirection sites can benefit from scale of use. Security is also of concern since site spoofing and URL manipulation can lead to a host of problems generally not present in fully contained sites. In practice, Commerce Server is not geared up to use this type of service without additional coding and development work.

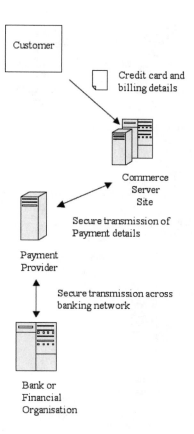

Figure 5.8
*Typical Commerce
Server payment
architecture.*

Customer

Credit card and
billing details

Commerce
Server
Site

Secure transmission of
Payment details

Payment
Provider

Secure transmission across
banking network

Bank or
Financial
Organisation

Ultimately, the final choice will depend on customer requirements, but remember that Commerce Server stops at the default payment component, and everything else will need to be written by the developers.

5.8 Commerce Server and BizTalk Server Integration

BizTalk Server is covered in detail in Chapter 4, but in essence it provides a message routing and translation gateway for business documents. Microsoft has worked to integrate BizTalk Server with Commerce Server so that orders that are placed on a Commerce Server site can be sent automatically by BizTalk Server to trading partners.

Imagine (if you will!) that your company sells lawnmowers and lawnmower parts. Some of the parts you build yourself, but others you order

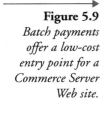

Figure 5.9
*Batch payments
offer a low-cost
entry point for a
Commerce Server
Web site.*

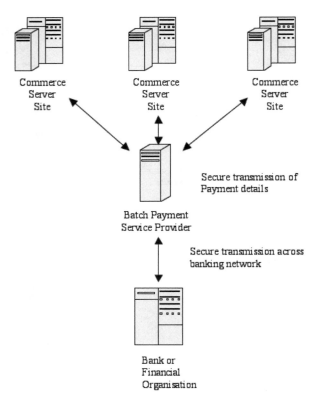

from trading partners. By creating a trading agreement with partners, when a visitor comes to your lawnmower site and places an order for a part supplied by that partner, Commerce Server will pass the order on to BizTalk Server, which will then package and send the order to the partner automatically. This process is transparent to the customer. If the item that is being ordered does not exist on the vendor site, an error message is generated on the destination server.

The catalog of parts from the trading partners can either be held as single catalogs or amalgamated into one larger catalog. The benefit of multiple catalogs is that it gives you more granular control over the products on your site and makes it easier to present different catalogs to different visitors (see Figure 5.10).

Each trading partner will have a unique ID, which, in turn, is displayed in the Commerce Server business desk. Vendors can have more than one catalog if need be.

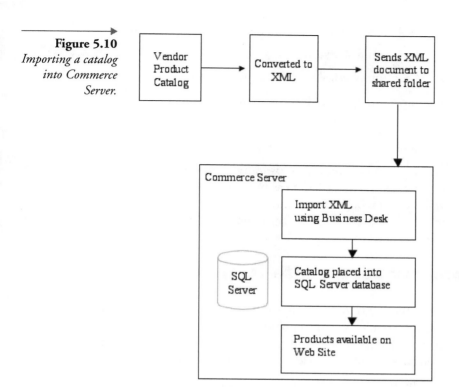

Figure 5.10
*Importing a catalog
into Commerce
Server.*

5.9   Managing a Commerce Server Installation

There are a range of monitoring tools that make the process of managing a Commerce Server site as straightforward as possible. The objective of monitoring a Commerce Server site should be to ensure that the site is available as required by the business and capable of servicing the visitors or customers to the site appropriately, bearing in mind that there will be peaks and valleys in the use of most sites. Data from the performance monitoring process, such as event logs and alerts, are stored in a SQL Server database for later analysis.

An important point to note is that performance monitoring will introduce an overhead on the site, and it is possible to overmonitor a site, so that performance is adversely affected.

Benchmark, or calibration, tests are often undertaken prior to a site being made available for public use to determine the capacity of the hardware. This is especially useful when using new hardware, that is unfamiliar or a new technology that you have not experienced before.

The benchmark tests should determine the following:

- Maximum disk bytes per second
- Maximum physical disk writes per second
- Maximum physical disk reads per second

Any later disk throughput can then be measured against these values.

The site usage profile needs to be monitored on a regular basis, and any new trends emerging—such as more users at certain times than expected—will need to be factored into any medium-term hardware upgrades to improve capacity. Conversely, if the usage profile is lower than expected, this will need to be flagged back into the business for remedial action.

5.10   Commerce Server Site Optimization

Once the site is live, then squeezing as much performance out of the site as possible should become an objective for you. The site, as with all IT installations of importance, will need to be fully documented and appropriate schematics should be created to assist in finding bottlenecks.

The transaction cost analysis (TCA) metric is often used to measure a site's capacity. In this case the transaction refers to work completed to fulfill a user request, such as placing an item into a shopping basket. It does not mean an exchange of funds to purchase something or a traditional database transaction. A base TCA is normally established before a site goes live using predicted site traffic to define a system benchmark.

6

Microsoft SQL Server

Without exception, every time we build a .NET solution, SQL Server will figure somewhere in the architecture owing to the requirement to persist or permanently store data in a structured format somewhere along the line. This can range from state and session information to storing product information from Microsoft Commerce Server 2002.

Many of the Microsoft .NET Enterprise Server products will use SQL Server by default. In some cases you could possibly switch this to Oracle or another database, but that would generally be more trouble than it's worth. Because of this, Microsoft SQL Server is becoming increasingly prevalent throughout many organizations.

6.1   SQL Server Architecture

Microsoft SQL Server comprises a number of areas of functionality, including the following:

- *Relational Database*—This is the SQL Server database engine and is where all of the data is stored in table-based structures. Data access is controlled by the relational database engine, and the clever use of indexes and data structures in this area increases the speed at which data can be retrieved (see Figure 6.1).

- *Administration*—Managing and controlling the database is done via the Enterprise Manager, which sits in the Microsoft Management Console application. Microsoft has done a fair bit of work in making the database as easy as possible to manage, and every task, such as backups, table creation, replication, and disk management, can now be completed from this interface. In the past, database administrators (DBAs) would have used the command-line interface and laboriously typed in commands on the screen (see Figure 6.2).

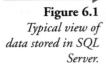

Figure 6.1
Typical view of data stored in SQL Server.

- *Replication*—Replication comes as standard in SQL Server and enables you to transfer data from one server to another on an automated basis. This is useful if you have a number of offices geographically split that need, for example, to receive product updates on a regular basis.

- *Data Warehousing and (OLAP)*—A data warehouse is used to store data in a read-only format that can be examined or mined by business experts to determine trends or patterns in the data set. OLAP, or *Online Analytical Processing* structures the data into multidimensional cubes, which can then be explored by analysis tools to understand, for example, who is buying which products in certain countries.

Figure 6.3 illustrates the major elements of SQL Server.

6.1.1   How SQL Server Stores Data

In the bad old days, SQL Server stored the physical data in device files with associated transaction files held on dump devices. Segments were used to span a database across multiple physical disks, which was extremely complicated. In fact, dump devices were a hangover from the Sybase UNIX product, and they were eliminated from SQL Server 7.0 onward.

Each SQL Server database has three file types:

1.   *Primary*—This file references other files and has the extension .mdf.

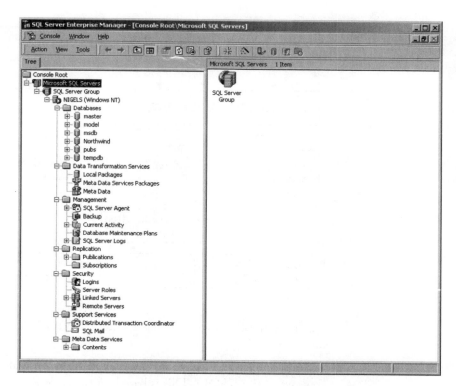

Figure 6.2
SQL Server Enterprise Manager.

2. *Secondary*—Data that is not held in the primary file is held in one or more secondary files with the extension .ndf.

3. *Log*—Logged information is used in database recovery, and a database will have at least one log file with the extension .ldf.

Files have an external "friendly" name and an internal logical name. SQL Server uses pages and extents for storage. A page is 8KB in size, producing 128 pages per megabyte.

6.1.2 SQL Server and Transact SQL

SQL—Structured Query Language—has been around in some form or other for a number of years now and is the usual way in which relational databases are accessed. In fact, with Microsoft SQL Server, regardless of which front end you decide to use against the database ultimately, a stream of SQL will be produced and sent to the database engine. This applies

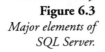

Figure 6.3
Major elements of
SQL Server.

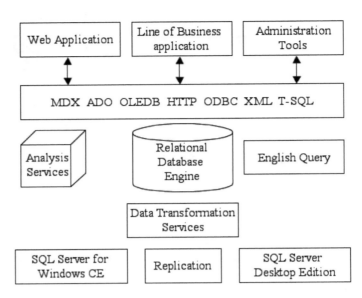

equally to the Enterprise Manager, Internet, Visual Basic, or any other client application.

Microsoft SQL Server has its own version or dialect of SQL called
Transact-SQL (T-SQL). This is based on the language standards defined by
the International Organization for Standardization (ISO) and the American
National Standards Institute (ANSI) in 1992. In fact, SQL Server 2000
supports Entry Level SQL-92, published (not surprisingly!) in 1992. By
way of comparison, Oracle uses a dialect of SQL called PL/SQL, which also
supports Entry Level SQL-92. Both of these products have SQL language
enhancements that are not considered standard to support specific database
features.

T-SQL does more than just retrieve data from the database, and is used
for the following:

- *Data definition*—creating the tables, relationships, and other structures for storing the data

- *Data retrieval*—allowing an application or user to retrieve data from
  the database

- *Data manipulation*—the updating or adding of data

- *Controlling access*—permitting users to log on to the server and carry out appropriate tasks

- *Maintaining data integrity*—creating constraints in the database, protecting it from data inconsistencies or breaches of business rules

- *Data sharing*—allowing users or groups of users to share data elements

6.1.3 Replication

As you probably know, replication is the process of taking data (or articles) from one server (the publisher) via a distribution server to subscribers. This allows data to be distributed according to business requirements and synchronized to ensure consistency. With merge replication, users can modify data and return it to the master server, where changes can be reconciled.

One use of this has been to implement transactional replication to copy each and every change to a master database to an off-site subscriber. This works by using the transaction log in SQL Server to detect each INSERT, UPDATE, DELETE, or other data modification, and then copying these to the subscribing backup server. This data transfer latency can be reduced to a few seconds if the appropriate network infrastructure is in place.

While this may be seen as an ideal solution for cheap standby servers, there are some catches. First, there is no transactional guarantee that the data has been copied over to your standby server. In other words, as the distribution server sends out the changes, there is no transactional confirmation that the changes have reached the standby server and that the data sets are in absolute synchronization. This means that if you do have a failure of your distribution server, you may have lost one or more transactions in the ether, depending on your replication latency.

Some businesses can accept this possible data loss as part of the cost/benefit analysis of this solution, but others will find this wholly unacceptable. On that basis, treat this solution with care, and maybe offer it to the business as a "warm standby" rather than a "hot standby" server.

6.1.4 SQL Server Performance and Availability

Performance, performance, performance. I know it's corny, but your competitor is "just one click away," and having a slow Web site is one sure way to push business to competitors. If we extract all the other possible performance bottlenecks from the Web solution and focus on the database, a number of performance-enhancing factors spring to mind.

A colleague of mine recently interviewed a developer and asked him about database normalization, and it was quite evident that even a senior developer was not aware of database design and the impact it has on performance. Normalization involves the removal of redundant, or duplicate, data from a database system. While this has definite upsides for efficient data storage, it results in data being distributed in separate tables. Each time your Web application submits a query (e.g., show me all the products that I have purchased over the past year), SQL Server has to work hard to join together data from, probably, the products, customer, and sales-history tables. During this process the optimizer needs to determine if it will be quicker to retrieve all of the product information and join that with the customer details, and then the sales history, or to retrieve the sales-history data and join that with the customer table, and then the products information, and so on and so on, until all the possible join combinations have been reviewed and the best strategy selected.

The number of possible join combinations is the factorial of the number of tables involved in the query, so the amount of work SQL Server has to do goes up with the number of tables in the query. This will result in SQL Server becoming bogged down with a tremendous amount of work in order to deal with (superficially) simple queries.

When we design the database for Web solutions, we will undertake a formal normalization process and follow that with tactical denormalization to deal with frequently accessed data sets.

Database I/O can have a significant impact on performance since the process of retrieving and submitting bytes to and from the storage subsystem takes a finite amount of time. If we assume that you have invested in decent, branded servers with loads of memory, a RAID set, and an excellent disk set controller, then we can look at the SQL Server considerations.

A useful feature in SQL Server is file groups. By grouping appropriate files together—for example, data files—into a single group, they can be managed as a single cohesive unit. This allows the DBA or developer to place the set of files onto a stripe set in a RAID configuration and reduce the amount of disk head movement to retrieve information. A typical Web site example may be placing a large product catalog into a file group alongside product-sales information. When users query product sales, the data will be retrieved from one file group.

One feature that will have an extreme influence on performance is correct index usage. Many Web solutions are fairly proscriptive in their functionality. For example, a B2C shopping site will be used by people browsing and, hopefully, purchasing products. This will involve entering search criteria or paging through product listings followed by the purchase action. You are very unlikely to allow ad hoc searching against random sets of data in this case. Part of the design work will be to identify the 15 or 20 query actions and then index to optimize.

Queries that are selective, which means they are likely to retrieve a small percentage of the table, lend themselves very well to nonclustered indexes. For example, when a user logs onto the site to place an order, you may wish to retrieve his or her previous orders. By having a nonclustered index, you would be able to retrieve the appropriate records without initiating an expensive table scan since the user first name + last name combination is reasonably selective, 90 percent of your customers happened to be named John Smith, which would initiate a table scan irrespective of the index since it takes less effort!

Clustered indexes force the data to reside in index order on the disk. As previously mentioned, reduction in I/O is generally a good thing; so reading sequential chunks of data during an index scan is often beneficial. The simplest analogy is the telephone directory, which is ordered in last-name order. In fact, a telephone directory is analogous to a composite clustered index since the first names are used for sorting within the last names. On that basis, if your Web site user wishes to search for a range of values (i.e., show me all the orders I placed between November and January), then, by applying a clustered index to the appropriate table, the results should be returned quicker. This may at times create a contradiction since you may need to choose between a clustered and nonclustered index. I would suggest that you choose an initial index, and then run the SQL Server Index Tuning Wizard after your site has been running for awhile to see if SQL Server requests an alternate based on the type of query traffic received.

6.1.5 Availability, Disaster Recovery, and Failover Clusters

Microsoft's own IT function reckons that 99.5 percent annual availability represents an acceptable commercial system. This equates to nearly 50 minutes downtime per week, per year. High availability is 99.9 percent to 99.99 percent availability, which equates to 10 minutes downtime per week, per year, and super high availability reduces this to even less downtime. Many customers we deal with can't accept any Web site downtime since it will affect business processes such as share trading.

Whenever we are designing a .NET system to withstand disaster, we always discuss a spectrum of likely solutions, ranging from large-scale, off-site storage and transaction management to simple tape-based backups. The deciding factor in all of these is always money, and businesses need to take a balanced view on the cost/benefit equation.

Interestingly, our customers are now considering disaster scenarios that would have previously been considered fantastic. Luckily, Microsoft SQL Server has some neat features that essentially build in good disaster recovery quite cheaply.

With Microsoft Cluster Services, a client can still access a SQL Server application if a server in a cluster fails since other servers in the cluster take up the workload automatically. The usual configuration is a two-node cluster with two SQL Servers working in an active/active combination. This means that each server undertakes its normal workload, but, in the event of failure, the remaining server takes on the additional workload of the failed server. With the SQL Server Datacenter product, it is possible to have up to four nodes in a cluster.

In the early days of clusters, the physical distance between servers was limited by the length of SCSI cable between them. This essentially placed the servers side by side in the same installation. With recent innovations in clusters and networking, this distance can now be significant, allowing a cluster to be distributed over two physically separate buildings, providing better disaster recovery. For example, with a Compaq Proliant HA/F500 cluster, you can have up to 100 km between nodes with Asynchronous Transfer Mode (ATM) or Gigabit Interface Converters (GBICs).

Unfortunately, there are some drawbacks with clusters. First, in an active/active combination, if both of the servers are working hard and one should fail, the remaining server is doing the work of both servers, which would obviously have a detrimental impact on performance. Second, when a server does fail for whatever reason, the failover process can take up to a minute or so since transactions are rolled back and the work load distributed to the second server. The user, in this instance, will see a pause in service and may need to reissue queries or updates once the failover has completed.

6.1.6   .NET and SQL Server Development

.NET provides the infrastructure for developing a new range of Web-based solutions and dominates everything that Microsoft now talks about. Web services are especially dominating the conversation since they have introduced a new way of building and deploying some pretty advanced solutions using a combination of XML and Simple Object Access Protocol (SOAP).

As far as SQL Server is concerned, life carries on much the same because much Web-based development is fairly remote from the day-to-day running of a SQL Server. Web-based applications are essentially inserting, updating, selecting and deleting data from the database. The major differences now are extra demands on the DBA to build scalable and very robust databases capable of providing 24/7 services to Web site users.

Undoubtedly this will change with the advent of YUKON, the next version of Microsoft SQL Server, which will then turn it into a "proper" .NET Enterprise Server. Until then, we will have to make do with the extra XML add-ons from Microsoft.

For the application developer, Web-based development has introduced a new set of challenges and choices when it comes to building solutions to work against SQL Server.

6.1.7 Connection Technologies

Over the years an alphabet soup of connection technologies has come and gone as the technology has matured from client/server to Web-based development.

These connection technologies include the following:

- DB-Library was the only way to build SQL Server client applications for a number of years. It is a C application programming interface (API) and allows access to all of the SQL Server features. It is still supported by Microsoft, but its longevity is in doubt because of the newer technologies in .NET.

- Open Database Connectivity (ODBC) was Microsoft's strategic data access API. It is based upon an open standard generated by the SQL Access Group (SAG) and was widely used by developers when building Visual Basic/SQL Server client/server applications in the mid-1990s because it made SQL Server and other databases more easily accessible than was previously the case. ODBC supposedly allowed an easy swap of databases since it used a generic API, which essentially abstracted the database specifics from the client application. The reality was often very different though, and many applications were rewritten to overcome database-specific problems.

- Remote data objects (RDO) overlays ODBC and was designed to give developers a lighter interface to SQL Server and Oracle and to enable the developer to use stored procedures and other RDBMS objects for improved functionality and performance. Data access objects (DAO) was used by Visual Basic developers to write applications that used ODBC.

- ActiveX Data Objects (ADO) is designed to be like both RDO and DAO. Its object model offers more flexible access to data types—from spreadsheets to relational databases. It achieves this by creating an object interface to OLE DB. OLE DB is a data access interface that uses complex structures and pointers, both of which would be beyond the scope of Visual Basic.

- Initially called SQL-OLE, SQL Server Distributed Management Objects (SQL-DMO) brings the world of objects to the management of SQL Server. SQL Server has an object model with 40+ separate objects containing 600+ interfaces. SQL DMO is implemented as a dual interface in-server process designed for developers who wish to create applications to undertake routine tasks or manage alerts, job execution, or SQL Server replication. SQL-DMO is not used to access any user data in the database.

6.1.8   Analysis Services and SQL Server

I have been fascinated by data warehousing for many years, ever since Microsoft introduced the CUBE and ROLLUP functions in SQL Server 6.5, enabling a T-SQL programmer to aggregate values into very simple result sets that could be used to analyze data trends. I also enjoyed telling great stories—or more likely urban myths—about the sales of beer and ale being intrinsically linked on a Friday night, when men were ordered to do the shopping for the weekend and took the opportunity to stock up on alcohol. This trend was, of course, discovered by analyzing or mining the store sales data in a data warehouse and serves to prove the commercial benefit of just such a system, or so the story goes.

A data warehouse is a read-only repository of subject-oriented data structured to enable efficient querying and analysis. Data is taken from operational systems and fed into the data warehouse via a data cleansing or scrubbing process. Once inside the data warehouse, the data is placed into tables, linked in such a way that predefined queries execute quickly and ad hoc queries run as speedily as possible.

Performance is critical to a data warehouse, as is the accuracy of the returned data since a failure in either aspect will lead to immediate disillusionment for the users.

6.2 Data Warehouse Data Structures

Relational databases typically use a cost-based optimizer. If a query contains multiple table joins or links, the optimizer will examine each combination of table joins in turn to determine the best execution plan. For example, a query, such as show me all of the sales of beer brand X in all Kwik-E-Mart stores for the past two weeks excluding London, would probably touch a products table, a stores table, a sales table, and a regions table in a conventional database schema.

This can lead to many combinations being examined—for example, a 4-table join has a total of four factorial (24) possible join combinations a 10-table join has an amazing 3,628,800 possible join combinations! The query optimizer in SQL Server 2000 has been tuned to try to overcome this multijoin problem, but the issue still exists and is subject to the limitations of the data structure.

Within a data warehouse environment, where a wide variety of queries can be executed, the designer needs to try to preempt the user by reducing these table joins. This is achieved by using a star or snowflake schema, amalgamating commonly used data into a single table.

Data merging to produce a star schema is a useful design tool when the following conditions are met:

- Tables share a common key.

- Data from the tables are used together on a frequent basis.

- Data insertion, if appropriate, is the same across the tables.

In fact, there is a slight difference between the star and snowflake structures since the snowflake structure has the surrounding dimension tables in a more normalized form.

6.3 OLAP, MOLAP, ROLAP, and HOLAP

On-line Analytical Processing (OLAP) is technology used to build and maintain data in a multidimensional format, such as a cube. The source data is often stored in an underlying relational database in traditional rows and columns, and the cube is built on top of that.

MOLAP is the name given to conventional cube or multidimensional OLAP structures. This offers fast query performance since the data is pre-built in the cube format, but often requires mass storage to store the aggregations—"data explosion" as it is called.

ROLAP is seen to be a more scalable solution and enables the data to remain in the SQL Server tables, with a skeletal cube structure is built to house the aggregations.

HOLAP is the use of a hybrid storage structure—that is, data that combines both ROLAP and MOLAP data. A good example of a hybrid solution is the use of regular reports, which analyze geographical data, but occasionally need to drill down into product-detail data. The geographical data is placed into a MOLAP cube and the product data placed into a ROLAP cube.

SLOWLAP is what you get when you do it wrong. OK, sorry about that—but I always have to get that pun in when talking about OLAP.

Table 6.1 lists the advantages and disadvantages of these technologies.

Table 6.1 *MOLAP? ROLAP? HOLAP? Which One Do I Use?*

	MOLAP	**ROLAP**	**HOLAP**
Advantages	■ Data navigation, slicing, and analysis are quicker since the dimensions have all been precalculated and stored	■ Data resides in the original data source, allowing changes to be reflected quicker ■ Cubes are quicker to process	■ Best of both worlds since the structure can be tuned to the business requirements for optimized performance
Disadvantages	■ Cube may take a while to process initially ■ Cube needs to be managed on a regular basis as new data come into the data warehouse.	■ Data navigation may be slower	■ Administration and management may be cumbersome

The cube is the central object in a multidimensional database containing dimensions and measures—dimensions being derived from underlying tables and columns and measures being the quantitative data derived from the columns. Dimensions should be distinct categories added to the cube. Measures are generally time periods or geographically-based metrics, which are often contained in a hierarchical structure—for example, hours roll into days, which roll into weeks.

The cube can hold a number of aggregations that can dramatically improve the efficiency and response time of a query. The scope of the aggregations can be massive, and the designer of a data warehouse needs to offset performance against storage space.

6.4   Data Mining and SQL Server Analysis Services

When building a data mining model, a set of training data needs to be collected that is based on accurate data from previous activities. For example, if you are selling SQL Server training courses, you collect the historical demographic data of course attendees and run that through your model to ensure that the results were as expected.

Once the training data has been assembled, the appropriate algorithm needs to be chosen. There are two data-mining algorithms used in analysis services, both of which are based on statistical theories that have been around for a number of years.

1.   Decision trees represent the data classification questions as nodes on a tree or a branch-like structure. The predictive nature of the algorithm is based on the training data set, influencing where the node is located and the depth of the node in the structure.

2.   Clustering, or the expectation method, groups data into clusters or neighborhoods of similar predictable characteristics. In many instances the clusters are counterintuitive and obscure, but that is the whole point of data mining!

The stored data-mining model is known as a model node, which contains detailed information, such as probabilities, attributes, and data descriptions. Within analysis services is a data model browsing tool, which visualizes the model content into something most people would understand.

Some of the real power of data warehousing is now being uncovered, as more and more organizations build Web sites that track a user's site journey and purchasing habits. When installed, Commerce Server builds a comprehensive data warehouse on the underlying SQL Server, which in turn can be used to analzse a range of user activities. If you haven't been asked to build a data warehouse yet, the chances are you will as the demand for business intelligence increases.

6.5   SQL Server Security

Microsoft SQL Server has been used for many years as a secure data repository, but with the product becoming increasingly mainstream, more and more organizations have a need to ensure that their databases are secure.

6.5.1   Modes, Modes, and More Modes

SQL Server 6.0 had three different security modes:

1.   Standard
2.   Integrated
3.   Mixed

Using standard security users would log onto SQL Server by specifying a login name and password. With integrated security, if the default named pipes protocol was used, users were automatically logged in to SQL Server using the Windows NT user name and login. This had the additional benefit of not sending the login/password combination across the network. Finally, mixed security was a mixture of standard and integrated security. If SQL Server uses protocols other than named pipes, mixed security will enable any user with either integrated or standard security to log into a SQL Server with a valid login name and password combination.

With SQL Server 7.0, Microsoft changed the security model. Windows NT authentication mode was introduced, which was similar to the previous integrated security mode in SQL Server 6.0. Mixed mode was retained and the old standard mode, which effectively ignored Windows NT security, was dropped.

Windows authentication and mixed mode are the two security models now used in SQL Server 2000. SQL Server authentication is retained in the mixed mode for backward compatibility reasons and because SQL Server running on Windows 9.*x* does not have access to Windows NT/2000 security.

Once a user has successfully logged in to SQL Server, he or she has passed the first security hurdle. The next step is for the user to have access to appropriate databases on that particular server. This is a useful feature, since permissions can be set at a fairly granular level from now on. A good example would be a developer who may be permitted access to a development database but not to the personnel database that also resides on the same server. Each user account in each database can also have appropriate object permissions assigned—for example, access to specific views or tables. If there is no specific account set up, then guest access can be permitted; the scope of that access is defined by the database administrator for such informal use.

6.5.2 Groups and Roles

Imagine having to set up 500 individual accounts, ranging from the CEO to the reception staff. Each user would need to be given database access tuned to his or her requirements. On a one-by-one basis this would be a time-consuming task that would drive most administrators up the wall. To deal with just such a scenario, SQL Server has the concept of groups and roles.

A group is a Windows NT or Windows 2000 administrative unit that contains individual users or other groups of users. A role is a SQL Server administrative unit that contains SQL Server logins, Windows 2000/NT logins, groups, or other roles.

Roles are normally created when there is no natural match between the existing Windows NT/2000 groups or when the database administrator does not have the rights to set up or manage such accounts. We often use this facility when a team of developers needs to access specific objects, such as tables in a database for a project. A user can belong to more than one role in a database at the same time, which is a useful feature.

6.5.3 Types of Users

Not all users would need to have the same rights in a database or SQL Server installation, so it is useful to have types of users who have different responsibilities and tasks to achieve.

The systems administrator (sa) has full rights throughout a SQL Server installation and can undertake any task in any database. In mixed mode the sa password is blank since SQL Server set up does not allocate a password. This needs to be one of the first items changed following installation; it is surprising to note the number of SQL Servers that still have a blank sa password. In Windows authentication mode, the sa password is already set since it is a SQL Server login. As expected, if you forget your sa password, the only remedy is a fresh reinstall. The sa role is actually called a fixed server role, since each and every SQL Server needs an sa. Other fixed server roles include serveradmin, setupadmin, and diskadmin.

The database owner (dbo) is a special user who has full rights within a particular database. Each member of the sysadmin fixed server role is mapped automatically to the dbo fixed database role.

Any user who is given permission by a dbo or sa to create an object in a database is called a database object owner. Once users have created their object, they can grant access to it to other users; this must be explicitly given for each user or set of users. This has implications regarding the way in which SQL Server references objects in a database since different users can create objects and then call them by the same name. Therefore, the formal name of each object in a database is the object owner followed by the object name. For example, if user Fred decides to create a table called customers_table, the table would be called

```
fred.customers_table
```

If the object owner name is not specified, SQL Server will raise an error—unless the object is owned by the current user or dbo.

As previously mentioned, the guest account is designed for users with a SQL login but no account in a specific database. If a database does have the guest account enabled, the user will automatically be granted the privileges assigned to that account, which is managed like any other SQL Server database account.

6.5.4   Security Account Delegation

This is a feature introduced in SQL Server 2000 that allows a user to login to a SQL Server and then have his or her credentials retained as he or she passes through a chain of SQL Servers. To implement security account delegation, Windows 2000 must be running on each server, with Kerberos security enabled and Active Directory implemented. The setup process is reasonably involved. Some Active Directory options need to be set, allowing the account and the computer to take part in the delegation. SQL Server must also have a service principal name assigned by Windows 2000, which proves that the server is running the correct installation of SQL Server at that specific socket address (hence, the reason why you must be running TCP/IP and not named pipes to support this feature). This involves running a utility from the Windows 2000 Resource Kit, a task best left to your domain administrator.

By following some logical, straightforward rules there is no reason why your installation of SQL Server should not be robust and secure enough for prime-time applications. Remember, most security violations are due to human failure rather than anything else.

Microsoft Content Management Server

Content management is the process of ensuring that a Web site contains relevant up-to-date material. The content needs to be created and submitted securely, with appropriate business approval, to ensure that it is suitable for use on a company's site. As well as attracting bad publicity, inaccurate content can lead to legal problems.

The need for content management came about soon after organizations built their own Web sites and realized that they needed an army of HTML authors just to keep the site up-to-date. As the number of Web site pages increased, so did the number of HTML authors since the process of designing and managing Web pages is fairly labor intensive. Clearly, this was

Figure 7.1
Before content management tools were developed, Web site authors would become an expensive bottleneck.

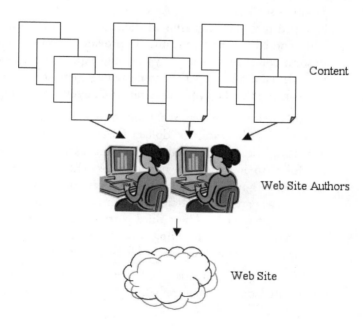

Content

Web Site Authors

Web Site

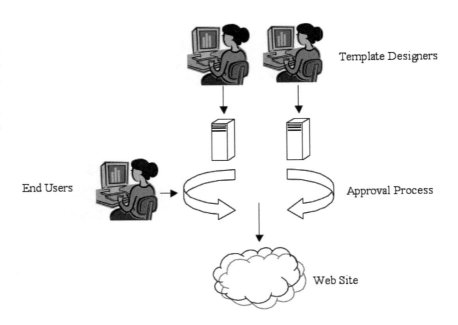

Figure 7.2
With content management products, templates are built and then any end user with appropriate rights can submit content.

Template Designers

End Users

Approval Process

Web Site

impractical, and the costs of such an operation were becoming too much for many organizations to bear (see Figure 7.1).

A number of organizations built home grown-solutions, some using products such as Microsoft Access and SQL Server. The site content would be typed into the database and then linked from the database to the site. This worked well and continues to provide a level of content management to some companies today. As you would expect, the dot-com boom led to a huge demand for "proper" content management solutions, and a number of companies started up providing just such a service (see Figure 7.2).

Although feature-rich, these solutions were very expensive, often costing hundreds of thousands of dollars for a basic implementation. In parallel with this, Microsoft realized that content management was missing from its portfolio, so it struck up relationships with some content management companies (notably NCompass and Interwoven) to provide content management as part of the Microsoft Commerce Server Business Desk application (see Chapter 5). These third parties were given the appropriate hooks and were able, with differing levels of success, to provide basic content management features for Microsoft-based Web sites.

Microsoft subsequently purchased NCompass and renamed the product Microsoft Content Management Server, launching it as part of the .NET Enterprise Server range.

Figure 7.3
*HTML
placeholders in
Content
Management
Server.*

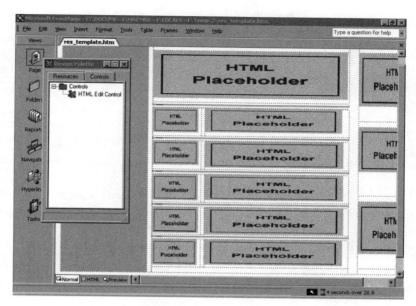

7.1 How Content Management Server Works

Microsoft Content Management Server uses Microsoft SQL Server as an object and data repository, linking graphics and text stored in the database to the Web pages. It uses a neat idea of page templates, which are built by experienced HTML authors, who then hand them over to the end users for updating with appropriate business or organizational data (see Figure 7.3).

7.2 Users in Microsoft Content Management Server

There are a number of user roles in Microsoft Content Management Server that have appropriate rights to do tasks and access appropriate containers, which are used to store Web site resources.

If you are using Windows 2000, users can automatically be imported into Microsoft Content Management Server every 15 minutes or so after the user logs in on Windows 2000. Therefore, any user with access to your Windows 2000 network is automatically made into a potential Microsoft Content Management Server user. To make better use of this feature, some organizations create a new Windows 2000 domain to manage user access more easily.

The Content Management Server user access rights are summarized in Table 7.1.

Table 7.1   *Content Management Server User Access Rights*

Role	Rights	Containers
Subscriber	■Browse pages published to channels that they have rights to	■No Site Builder access
Author	■Create, edit, and submit pages in folders ■Create and submit postings in channels ■Use the page template ■Use resources	■Folder ■Template gallery ■Resource gallery ■Channel
Editor	■Approve pages ■Delete pages ■Edit postings ■Create pages in folders and submit postings in channels ■Use the page template ■Use resources	■Folder ■Template gallery ■Resource gallery ■Channel
Moderator	■Modify posting schedules ■Approve postings	■Channel
Resource Manager	■Add, remove, and replace content in a resource gallery	■Resource gallery
Template Designer	■Design page and navigation resources ■Use resources	■Template gallery ■Resource gallery
Administrator	■Assign users, rights, and roles ■Create hierarchies ■Assign rights in containers	■Folder ■Channel ■Template gallery ■Resource gallery ■User roles

7.2.1   **Containers**

Containers are workspaces or directories where users complete their tasks depending on their appropriate role.

Microsoft Content Management Server containers are

- Folders—used to store pages
- Channels—used for postings
- Galleries—used for templates and resources

Any typical Content Management Server–based site is actually built up from a number of elements, including:

- *Page templates*—These allow authors to build Web site pages without writing HTML since the content is written directly into the pages via placeholders. The properties of the placeholders are set by the template designers, who decide what a user can and can't add in a particular place on a page. The authors' menus are changed dynamically to reflect precisely what they can and can't do in a placeholder.

- *Navigation templates*—These are used to make site navigation easier for users when the site is being managed through a Web browser. They provide a hierarchy of channels and order of pages added to the channels. In most cases they will also include Help and Home buttons.

- *Postings*—Publishing a page in Microsoft Content Management Server is the process of posting it to a channel with a publishing schedule. The publishing schedule will have page expiration dates and channel information. Typically, a page will be expired if, for example, it contains a special offer that only lasts a set time.

- *Folders*—Folders are used to store Microsoft Content Management Server pages. Therefore, every channel must have an associated folder. An editor will have one or more folders assigned and is responsible for approving the pages before they are published. If a folder does not have an editor, then any pages submitted to the folder will automatically be published. Likewise, if a folder is used to store pages created by its own editor, then the pages will be autoapproved.

- *Channels*—Channels organize postings into a hierarchy and are used to store, organize, and manage access to content. Any content posted to a channel can only be published after a moderator has approved it.

7.2.2 Authoring a Page

Adding content to a page in Microsoft Content Management Server is fairly straightforward.

The authoring process is started by a user logging into the Microsoft Content Management Server Site Builder application with a user name and password. An appropriate view will then be created, depending on the user's role within that Web site. The authoring and publishing process is often in a state of flux since a number of users can be making changes at any moment in time—so the site pages are assigned state information to keep track of who is doing what to the various pages.

The state information provided will include the following:

- *New*—The page is brand new and being worked on for the first time. It has not been saved before within Microsoft Content Management Server.

- *Saved*—The page has been saved to the system, but not submitted for approval.

- *Waiting*—The page has been sent for approval, but not approved by the editor.

- *Approved*—The page has been approved by an editor.

- *Declined*—The page has been turned down by an editor and has not been modified and resubmitted.

- *Expired*—The page has been approved, but has expired since the expiration time set on the page is earlier than the current time.

Microsoft Content Management Server uses a basic locking model to ensure that only one user can edit a page or object at a time. Any other users will be able to work with the page or object as read-only.

If a user fails to release the object properly after editing, normally following a client machine being turned off while editing, the object can remain open and locked. To overcome this, Microsoft Content Management Server has a command called "Kill Lock," which does exactly as it says and will remove the lock from the object. Obviously, care needs to be exercized with this command because it can corrupt or lose data if used incorrectly.

7.2.3   Template Families

Template families are used to create multiple views of any one page. Every page is based on at least one template, but an author can create a second view of the same page by using a second template. The content of each of the views can have common shared elements or can be different.

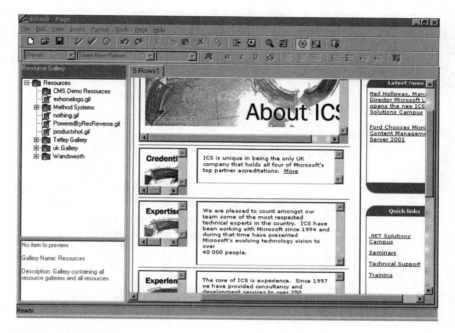

Figure 7.4
Page editing.

7.2.4 Page Editing

If a user has editor rights, he or she can edit, approve, decline, or delete pages submitted to the folders. As part of the approval process, if a page is declined a note can be added explaining why it was declined and giving suggestions for any changes (see Figure 7.4).

7.2.5 Page Revisions and Versioning

Microsoft Content Management Server supports versioning and revisions. Revisions are based on postings, and any changes to a posting are not versioned. But changes of a posting's page, template, or resource gallery can be viewed as revisions of a posting that does use them.

Unapproved pages have the date and time a revision was last modified alongside the page status. Approved revisions have the date and time the revision was approved, the type of the revision, and the name of the person who made the revision. There is also the option to preview and compare the revisions.

Revisions can be stored according to the size of the Microsoft Content Management Server SQL Server database, so there is no hard limit.

There will be a requirement to do some basic database management in SQL Server. Maintenance, such as purging old revisions that you have stored, is a good idea, but be careful about doing this when the system is busy because it may end up locking users out during the clear down. Common sense would naturally come into play when managing your database, and having access to a SQL Server Database Administrator (DBA) can sometimes be useful.

7.2.6 Resources

Resources are mostly multimedia (i.e., graphics, videos) files that can be added to Web pages by users if they have rights to the resource gallery. Resource managers and administrators have read/write access to the resource galleries, and all other users have read-only access.

The following file types are supported in the resource galleries:

- GIF
- JPEG/JPG
- PNG
- ASF/ASX (Netshow videos)
- AVI
- MPEG/MPG
- MOV/QT (Quick Time)

Other resource formats can be used, but the file will be displayed as a link/attachment, and there is no guarantee how the file will be displayed or consumed by the browser. For example, a Word document will be viewed as a link, and unless the browser has a Word reader, the user will be prompted to save the file to disk or choose an application to run it.

Browsers that do not support any of the video images may need additional downloaded add-ins.

A useful feature of Microsoft Content Management Server is the ability to generate a dependent report on a resource so that you can see any pages that are consuming the resource and work out the ramifications should you delete it.

Users can also be caught out if they see that a resource is available, but have not refreshed their Site Builder application and so are not aware that, in fact, it has been deleted. To help with this, users should be encouraged to refresh Site Builder on a regular basis, and it may also be a good idea to move resources to another temporary archive for a day or two prior to deletion just to be sure.

7.2.7   Moderators

Moderators have rights to approve or decline postings in their channels. The publication schedule for the view of a page and its channel is set by a posting, so the moderator can decide if appropriate information is going to be published. The moderator actually uses a tool called the Approval Assistant, which returns up to 500 items that are awaiting approval in a search. Here the posting can be previewed in the moderator's browser.

7.2.8   Publishing and Content Delivery

One major benefit with Microsoft Content Management Server is the ability for anyone in an organization to write content for the Web site. Since Microsoft Content Management Server is database driven, all of the Web site content can be called up from the database, assembled on the page, and then displayed to the user. Images, such as logos, just need to be stored once and can then be accessed from numerous Web pages. If the logo is to be changed, it can simply be updated in the database.

Site authors access the usual Web site, but when they log in, they get access to additional menus and publishing tools. Web site editing is carried out in placeholders, which have been created on the page templates, so that anyone can edit text directly or drag-and-drop content, assuming he or she has the appropriate access rights.

7.2.9   Publishing Workflow

The publishing workflow for pages is quite straightforward. Authors use the Web Author tools to create a page and then set the posting or publishing schedule, which then determines when the content can be viewed. A posting will have a publishing schedule with start and expiration dates for a page and information about the channel to be used for publication (see Figure 7.5).

The channel will have stored the postings into a hierarchy, and when the author says so, the page will be submitted to the editor for approval. The

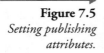

Figure 7.5
*Setting publishing
attributes.*

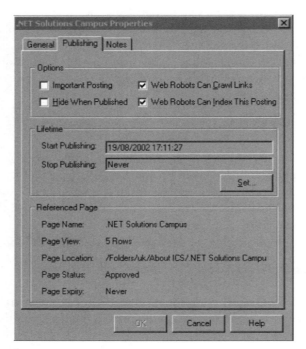

editor then approves the page, and the moderator will then check the content to ensure that it is appropriate for the channel.

The approval process can be based on either one or many individuals approving content that has been submitted.

- *Serial approval* is a vertical workflow that requires approval of content at each stage. If an editor fails to approve a page at his or her stage, then the page will never reach the Web site (see Figure 7.6).

- *Parallel single approval* allows content to be submitted to a number of approvers, any one of whom is authorised to approve content. Once the content has been approved by this one individual, it will automatically be removed from the other approvers' workload and forwarded to the next stage (see Figure 7.7).

- *Parallel all approval* is an extension of parallel single approval, and in this case all of the approvers would need to approve the content before it moves to the next stage. If any one approver refuses to clear the content, it will not move on to the next stage (see Figure 7.8).

Figure 7.6
Serial approval.

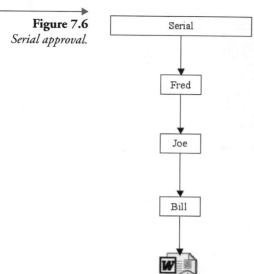

Figure 7.7
Parallel single approval.

Figure 7.8
Parallel all approval.

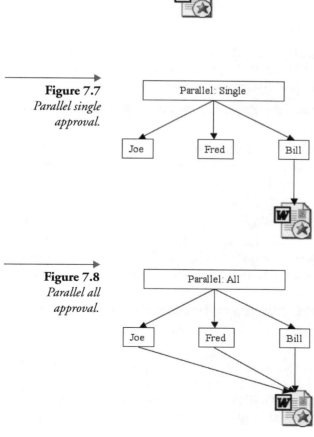

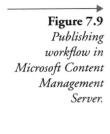

Figure 7.9
*Publishing
workflow in
Microsoft Content
Management
Server.*

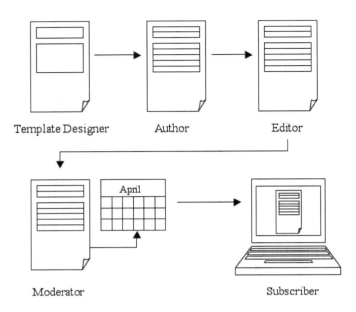

Template Designer   Author   Editor

Moderator   Subscriber

Once fully approved, the page's content will be published according to its start and expiration dates. If the expiration date is reached, the content will no longer be published to that channel.

Figure 7.9 illustrates the publishing workflow in Microsoft Content Management Server.

It is possible to publish pages consecutively so that you can create a new version of a page to replace an original on a specific date. This might be useful if you have a specific promotion starting on a set date that you wish to advertize on the Web site. Likewise, it is possible to publish channels consecutively.

Additionally, if you have pages that you wish to have published directly by the author without editor or moderator approval, just don't assign an editor to a channel's folder or a moderator to the channel. Microsoft Content Management Server will then autoapprove any postings that are submitted.

7.3   Microsoft Content Management Server and Site Staging

There are times when a static version of a Microsoft Content Management Server Web site is required—for example, if you wish to deploy the site on multiple platforms such as UNIX or LINUX. The Site Stager is designed to take Microsoft Content Management Server content and automatically

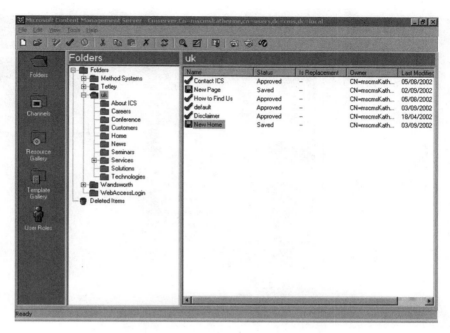

Figure 7.10 *Site Stager in Microsoft Content Management Server.*

convert it into HTML and ASP format files. In addition, it is used to separate the development and test environment from the final online server site, creating a separate publishing and browsing architecture. This use can be extended further, and the Site Stager can be used to create different Web sites with different content for specific users, fed from a parent or master site. This may be useful if you want to build, for example, a customer-specific site for all your retail customers, which would be different from a finance site (see Figure 7.10).

7.4   Server Configuration Application (SCA)

The Server Configuration Application is used to make changes to configuration values for a Microsoft Content Management Server installation. As expected, it is an administrator's tool only since it can make changes to database configurations that will impact the entire Web site.

Microsoft Content Management Server stores some system settings in the server registry, but most of the settings are actually table driven since they are stored in Microsoft SQL Server.

Typical Server Configuration Application tasks include the following:

Figure 7.11
*Server
Configuration
Application.*

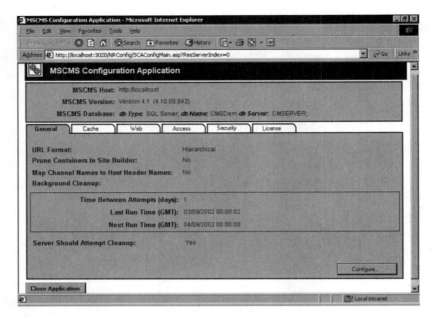

- Managing Windows NT domains
- Turning guest accounts on and off
- Changing Microsoft Content Management Server system accounts
- Changing the size of the memory cache
- Changing the size and location of the disk cache

The Server Configuration Application cannot change the Microsoft Content Management Server SQL Server from one server to another—neither can it change the SQL Server database being used by Microsoft Content Management Server (see Figure 7.11).

7.5 Site Deployment Manager

The Site Deployment Manager uses an import/export feature to update your Microsoft Content Management Server installation selectively. This allows the creation of a separate deployment and production server configuration.

Microsoft Content Management Server allows a number of objects to be transferred between servers:

- Channels and postings

- Folders

- Pages

- Resources and resource galleries

- Templates and template galleries

- User groups and group members

In addition to using the Site Deployment Manager, Microsoft Application Center Server also provides the means to transfer content between servers. For further information on Application Center Server, see Chapter 8.

Microsoft Content Management Server only supports the export of an object and its dependents. In other words, if you have a page with images on it, the pages and image file will always be transferred together, but only if they are in the Microsoft Content Management Server database. Dependent objects outside of the database (e.g., in a file directory) will not be moved automatically and must be copied manually.

The Site Deployment Manager has no ability to share objects that it is transferring, so it is possible to lock out users from the system when using it; therefore, it makes sense to use the tool at low-use times.

The Microsoft Content Management Server Site Deployment Manager is only used for transferring small numbers of objects from one server to another. If you wish to copy an entire site, SQL Server replication needs to be used.

Replication is the process of copying and distributing data between databases. This can happen between SQL Servers, handheld devices, and a SQL Server—via the Internet, network, or with local dial-up access. This flexibility has enabled organizations to build fairly complex replication models and is the basis of transferring large amounts of data between Content Management Server databases.

SQL Server uses a publisher and subscriber model for replication. A publisher will make data (i.e., site content) available in the form of articles for replication. An article can be as small as one row from one column or as large as complete tables or indexed views. The underlying data can be partitioned horizontally or vertically to produce an article. The publisher publishes the articles, which are read by subscribers to those articles. In complex or high-volume replication topologies, a publisher can be used to send articles to a separate distribution server, which will then carry the workload of sending out the articles.

7.6   Development and Production Servers

For most sites, other than the smallest, it would probably make sense to separate the development and production servers to two or more separate machines. While increasing hardware and software costs, this does allow far better quality control and management of the site.

Normally the site would be created on the first development server and then the Site Deployment Manager would be used to move the site structure to a second development server. The second server is used just for content development work, such as authoring and editing, with subsequent changes to the site structure being completed on the first development server and then copied to the second—again, using the Site Deployment Manager. These structural changes will be synchronized, leaving the content intact. The content is then moved to the production server using the Site Deployment Manager.

For content that carries regularly changing data that needs to update the Web site frequently (e.g., stock information or press releases), create a channel to hold the postings and then just move that across to save time.

7.7   Web Crawlers and Microsoft Content Management Server

Most organizations would like their public sites to be crawled and indexed by Web crawlers since this enables the site to be found from the popular search engines. Web crawlers generally work by taking the top-level pages submitted and then running through all of the links they can find. End-user search results are resolved from these stored pages or links.

Microsoft Content Management Server enables search engines to index any URLs that are accessible to guests visiting the site, and it is possible to add your own site search engine with access rights to index secure pages. Microsoft Content Management Server uses specific redirects, which may not be compatible with the Web crawler. If that is the case, HTML will need to be added to the template pages to ensure they are dealt with correctly.

7.8   Building a Site with Content Management Server

Most of the effort in building a Microsoft Content Management Server–based Web site is spent during the planning phase. In my experience, up to

60 percent of the project time can be used working through the issues of how the site developers work with the content owners and content managers. The political impact of defining organizationwide standards on a high-profile project, such as a Web site, can be significant. It seems that everyone wants to have a say on how the site works!

Having worked on a number of Microsoft Content Management Server projects, I know that the reality of building and deploying Microsoft Content Management Server is sometimes different from that laid out in Microsoft documentation.

As with all development work, any Microsoft Content Management Server site plan needs to be accompanied by a suitable methodology and an agreed set of deliverables. This would typically include such areas as the content plan, site navigation, templates, workflow, and deployment specifications.

Some of the content is likely to be dynamic, such as a news feed, and this requires management different from more static data sources, such as an about page or contact information.

7.8.1   Building a Content Plan

The content plan identifies the type of content that will be included in the site. This then feeds the Microsoft Content Management Server page templates and the navigation specifications. The site developers will then need to review the content plan to ensure that any pages to be ported across from an existing site are transferable and won't bring a host of problems along with them.

7.8.2   Navigation Specifications and Links

The navigation specification plans the links used to access the various parts of the site. Microsoft Content Management Server navigation is built on the fly, and new pages can be automatically linked based upon rules defined in the navigation specifications. There are three types of navigation:

1.   Global navigation refers to the top-level channels on any site.

2.   Local navigation refers to navigation within each top-level channel.

3.   The breadcrumb trail leaves a visible trail of where a user has visited on a site, enabling quicker user orientation. (The term bre*ad-crumb trail* is alleged to have come from the trail of breadcrumbs left by Hansel and Gretel so that they could retrace their steps in the fairytale forest. Certainly some Web sites are very much like a forest!)

7.8.3　Template Specifications

Most of the authors contributing to the site using Microsoft Content Management Server will, by their very nature, be nonexpert users of HTML and, on that basis, need to be guided through the content submission process. Using the content plan, each template needs to be defined with a name, use, and gallery reference. The style and content of each placeholder or field is then worked out—for example, stating that a name placeholder must be text only and bold. The functionality is then documented and the appropriate links laid out.

7.8.4　Workflow Specifications

As you should have seen by now, Microsoft Content Management Server has a set of workflow features that enables content to be published. By default, the out-of-the-box workflow is reasonably straightforward, and the general advice is to use this as it stands. If the workflow becomes too complex, pages can get lost in the approval process—never to be seen again. If you have Windows 2000 Active Directory or Windows 2000/NT users and groups enabled, the chances are that these can be mapped to Microsoft Content Management Server roles quite easily. Failing this, new groups and users may need to be set up. At this point drawing up a tabular diagram with roles mapped from Windows 2000/NT to Microsoft Content Management Server is probably the simplest thing to do.

7.8.5　Deployment

This defines how a site will be developed, staged, and deployed with all of the associated network and server technicalities. Areas considered include security, bandwidth, clustering, load balancing, and firewalls. When creating the deployment specification, workloads need to be considered and any final technical "gotchas" eliminated since it will be difficult to fix problems further down the line.

Complex sites will have separate development, test, staging, and production Microsoft Content Management Server sites all linked together to form the site. The costs associated with this type of implementation can be considerable in terms of both hardware and software, so think carefully about how your site is going to be structured and ensure that you secure a big enough budget from the start.

8

Microsoft Application Center Server

Running a Web site can be notoriously difficult since it entails balancing a set of requirements, such as scalability, manageability, hardware costs, and availability. As the number of users of the site increases, so does the success or failure of the site in the minds of businesspeople. Unfortunately, a Web site manager can never provide a satisfactory service in the minds of many people—any technical successes are generally hidden from the day-to-day users—but believe you me, when the Web site fails, everyone knows about it.

To assist in the management of a Web site, Microsoft released Microsoft Application Center Server, which is designed to offer better levels of manageability, scalability, and availability out of the box. Application Center has a set of tools that creates and manages a cluster of servers containing identical content, and with load balancing these tools ensure that demand for the application is spread evenly across these clustered servers (see Figure 8.1).

8.1   The Abilities

What is meant by the three "abilities" addressed by Microsoft Application Center Server? These are scalability, manageability, and availability.

8.1.1   Scalability

This is covered in more detail in Chapter 10, but in summary, scalability is the capacity for an application or Web site to cope with increasing numbers of, typically, concurrent users. Within applications, bottlenecks will often appear, as more users are added and the servers or components start to stress and choke due to the demand for data or resources. This will manifest itself in a Web site as slow response or generally poor performance. For the Web site administrator, this will manifest itself as a phone call from his or her boss!

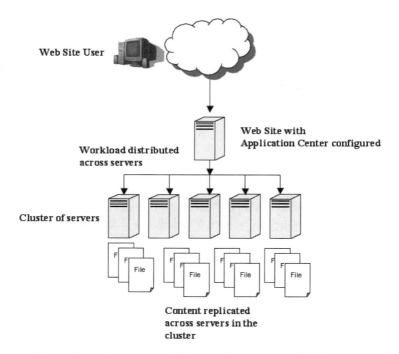

Figure 8.1
*Application Center
Server balancing
workload and
content.*

There is an important difference between scalability and performance. Many applications are deemed to be high-performance (e.g., processing many transactions per second), but as soon as you add extra users the application will slow. I have has seen cases of applications where increasing the users from 5 to 10 would destroy any level of performance. Although 10 users does not seem to be many, when users are selecting or updating large amounts of data the volume of database locks can increase dramatically, as can the requirement to serve up the all important session state information, often stored in the database as well.

8.1.2   Manageability

One "ability" that Microsoft generally excels at is manageability. It has done a good job of bringing toolsets that make complex server-based products easier to use than in the past. The strangely named "wizards" in many Microsoft products make setting up server applications a case of pointing and clicking, so many of the previously difficult or time-consuming tasks are now semiautomatic. That said, there are many cases when a wizard will run out of steam and only the intervention of an experienced administrator can save the day. Application Center uses the notion of a snap-in management tool with a set of wizards to manage and set up clusters and deploy content. In addition, it has a set of tools that support remote browser-based administration and, for the real diehards, a command line interface. An Application Center application is actually the content that a cluster will serve to site clients, and it will have all of the components and configuration settings needed to serve the content. A significant benefit of Application Center is that it keeps all of the disparate components of a Web site together in a single logical unit, which makes the deployment and subsequent management of a site much easier, including deployment across additional servers in the cluster. All of the associated logs of member servers in a cluster are automatically rolled into a single view of a cluster, making the process of clusterwide administration even easier.

8.1.3   Availability

This represents the last of our "abilities." There is little point in having a scalable, well-managed site if it is off-line and unavailable to users. To ensure the site is available, Application Center uses clusters of servers to remove any single point of failure. If any server member of a cluster should fail, the remaining members will pick up the workload and continue to make the site available. Monitoring tools within Application Center will detect failures and then trigger a range of responses as determined by the site administrator.

8.2   The Cluster

By bringing a number of servers together to work as a single unit, we have seen that single points of failure can be avoided. This cluster of servers is not a particularly new innovation, but its application in a Web-based product from Microsoft is. Previously, clusters were mainly used in database products, such as Microsoft SQL Server, or mail servers, such as Exchange. Application Center clusters are broader, since they are designed to deal with the Web tier, serving HTTP-based clients, and the business tier, which serves the COM-based business logic (see Figure 8.2).

There are three types of clusters supported by Application Center Server:

1.   General (Web tier) cluster

2.   COM+ application cluster

3.   COM+ routing cluster

Figure 8.2
Application Center
cluster.

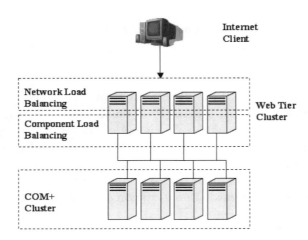

8.2.1   General Cluster

This is the conventional cluster that readers may be familiar with since it provides servers to manage a range of client requests and can include database, e-mail, and Web servers (see Figure 8.3).

Figure 8.3
The general Web
cluster.

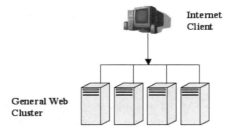

8.2.2   COM+ Application Cluster

This manages any method calls to instantiate business logic objects. These calls are load-balanced across cluster members to improve throughput. The COM+ application cluster deals exclusively with this type of load balancing (see Figure 8.4).

8.2.3   COM+ Routing Cluster

This will use component load balancing (CLB) to route any requests for COM+ components. In reality this would rarely be used, since Web clusters can communicate directly to back-end COM+ clusters, acting as their

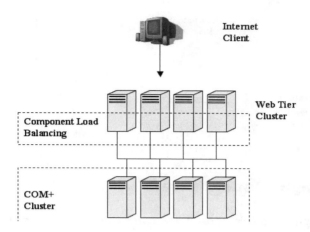

Figure 8.4
*COM+ application
cluster.*

own router to determine the best server to activate for component use (see Figure 8.5).

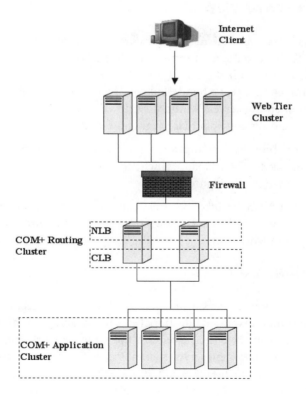

Figure 8.5
*COM+ routing
cluster.*

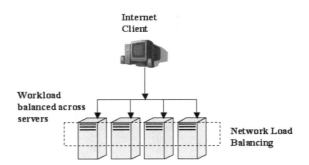

Figure 8.6
*NLB balancing
workload across
multiple servers.*

8.2.4   Single-Node Clusters

Application Center can be run on a cluster of one server or member. While
not suitable for a production environment, it can be used as a stager, where
content is placed onto a staging server. The content can then be fully tested
before moving it across to the production environment.

8.2.5   Standard Web Clusters

This is probably the most common use of Application Center Server, where
the Web cluster is used to serve both the Web site and COM+ components
held locally with the use of a load-balancing system, such as NLB. This is
useful since it will provide failover, so that if a member server should fail,
the remaining servers would pick up the workload, since they are all copies
of the cluster controller (see Figure 8.6 and 8.7).

Scalability is also improved since other servers can be added to the cluster to take on workload, which, in turn, will hopefully deliver improved
performance (see Figure 8.8).

Non-NLB balanced clusters can still be built, but would use another
load-balancing device from a list of supported third-party solutions available from Microsoft.

8.2.6   Building a Cluster

A cluster will always start from a single server (in effect a cluster of one) and
then build outward as additional servers are added to the cluster set. Assuming that you have the servers on the same network and they can see each
other, adding a new server to a cluster is fairly straightforward and should
be completed using the Add Cluster Member Wizard. The original server is
called the cluster controller and must start the cluster build process with all

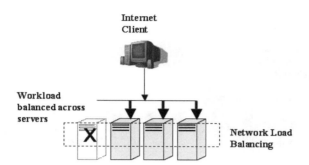

Figure 8.7
*Failover—the site
continues to be
available as other
member servers
pick up the
workload.*

of the site content and configuration material in a complete state. If you have decided not to use NLB, then each member cluster server must have its IP address bound to the cluster controller.

Most Application Server clusters will need to have the client and cluster communications configured. Client communication is normally done via a load-balancing mechanism to spread the load across multiple servers. Cluster communications are put in place to ensure that Application Center can send management requests between cluster members to synchronize content and administer the cluster. As you would expect, all of the networking issues need to be resolved before using the New Cluster Wizard, since changing network settings after the cluster has been built will probably require a complete rebuild of the cluster.

8.3   How NLB Works

Normally, the Application Center Wizard would be used to set up and configure NLB. Each member server must have at least two network adapters; one of which looks after client communication, while the other handles communications inside the cluster group.

Incoming client requests for TCP and UDP protocols, such as HTTP, are distributed across the cluster members using a software-based load-balancing mechanism. Member servers send an NLB exchange message over the load-balancing adapters about every second; this is used to coordinate actions between the cluster members. Any failure of these message exchanges will cause up to five retry attempts, after which any nonresponsive servers force Application Center to assume a server is not available. The workload is then distributed across the servers Application Center has had a response from, and any nonactive servers are automatically excluded from further work.

Figure 8.8
Adding additional servers will see the workload automatically redistributed across the cluster.

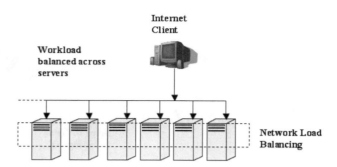

By default all member servers receive the workload coming into the cluster, but an algorithm decides which server actually processes the request, with the other servers discarding the workload. This architecture is actually faster than presorting the work for one server to undertake.

Affinity

A problem often found with load balancing is that of affinity. By definition the Web is a disconnected environment, so session state is often managed by the Web server. This is all very well when the client knows that it will be returning to the same server each time another HTTP round trip is made, but with load balancing this level of affinity needs to be explicitly managed since the client can return to any of the cluster servers, potentially losing session state.

NLB comes with three types of client affinity to preserve the all important session state information. These are as follows:

1. None—Multiple requests from a client can access any member server in the cluster. This provides the best level of performance but will probably disrupt clients with established sessions, since any further requests will often hit other cluster server members that do not have the session information.

2. Single—Multiple requests from a client must access the same member. NLB will use the client's IP address to ensure that subsequent responses are dealt with by the original cluster server member.

3. Class C—Multiple requests from the same TCP/IP class C address range must access the same cluster server member. This is normally utilized when using NLB to serve an Internet Web site.

8.4   Component Load Balancing (CLB)

CLB is used by Application Center Server to load balance requests for COM+ applications by balancing the activation requests coming into the Web site. This is covered in more detail in Chapter 10.

8.5   Request Forwarding

We have already seen that there are some distinct benefits to load balancing since the workload can be spread across multiple servers to improve performance and scalability. But what happens if we must ensure that some requests are only dealt with by, for example, the cluster controller? There is little point in sending a request to have a configuration changed just to see it disappear into a cluster member and not be seen by the controller. Likewise, if you have a client that has already established session state with a member server, there needs to be a mechanism to force the request to go to one server and one server alone.

This forced direction of requests is called request forwarding. The request forwarder manages session state by using cookies to tie a client to a particular cluster server member. Each time a subsequent request is submitted, the cookie is examined and the appropriate server receives the request.

As we have seen previously, all cluster members receive the workload, but only one server is told by the controller to action the work, while the others will discard it. Request forwarding will add another layer of work to this scenario since the requests will need to be processed, after they have been load balanced; therefore, the site will incur a performance penalty. To reduce the performance penalty, request forwarding can be turned off for specific file types.

8.6   Applications and Application Center

An application, as far as Microsoft Application Center is concerned, is a list of various resources and components that are synchronized or deployed in a cluster. Essentially, when you undertake a deployment, Application Center will look at the list of resources and ensure they are deployed according to the configuration rules.

The application can consist of a number of elements, including the following:

- COM+ applications
- File directories and files
- System data source names
- Registry keys
- Web sites, including all of the files, certificates, ISAPI filters, and certificate trust lists

By default, Application Center will create some applications when it is installed. These are designed to make the administration of clusters and Web applications easier.

Most applications that an Application Center administrator will be using will consist of a number of .NET-based resources, and Application Center Server will allow much better granular control over files that are distributed across the cluster of servers.

8.6.1   Automatic Synchronization

Application Center Server has two types of automatic synchronization that enable content to remain up-to-date across the servers on the cluster.

1.   With change-based synchronization Application Center receives notification if all but a few elements of content change (the exceptions being COM+ applications, CAPI store information, network settings, and access control list [ACL] changes). Once the notification is received, all of the clustered servers will be updated (see Figure 8.9).

- Interval-based synchronization uses a preset interval to undertake a full synchronization of the servers. The default setting is 60 minutes, but this can, of course, be changed (see Figure 8.10).

8.6.2   Manual Synchronization

This is essentially on-demand synchronization and allows a synchronization event to be forced across the participating servers. There are three types of manual synchronization.

1.   Member synchronization is used when only a specified member server of the cluster needs to be updated and will occur whether

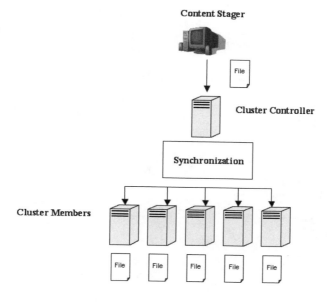

Figure 8.9
Change based synchronization.

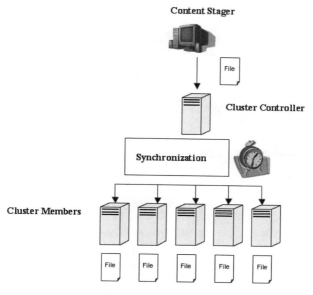

Figure 8.10
Interval-based synchronization with timed updates.

or not the server is in the formal synchronization cluster servers (see Figure 8.11).

2. Cluster synchronization forces an update to all members of the server cluster (see Figure 8.12).

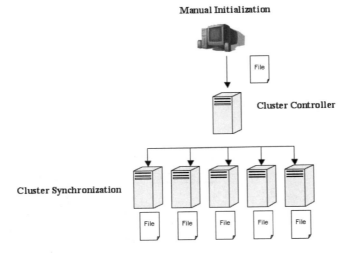

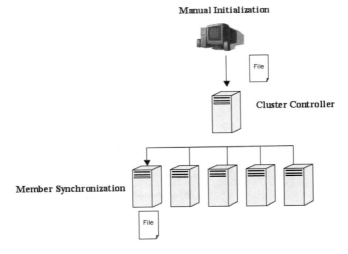

3.   Application synchronization ensures that a specified application is synchronized on every member of the cluster (see Figure 8.13).

The administrator can at any time prevent individual files, file types, folders, or content from being synchronized.

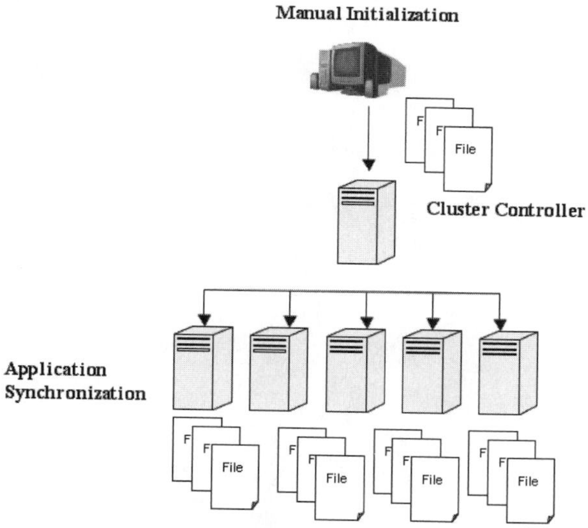

Figure 8.13
Application synchronization.

8.7 Monitoring a Solution Using Application Center Server

Once a cluster has been commissioned, the cluster administrator will need to use Application Center tools to monitor the cluster activities. The type of monitoring will probably focus around two of our core set of "abilities"—scalability and availability. Luckily, this monitoring is made easier since Application Center Server will automatically provide a set of charts and graphs that are easily interpreted. This information will come from a number of sources, including Windows 2000 events, Microsoft Health Monitor data collectors, and Application Center Server.

Data that is collected by Application Center Server is stored in a SQL Server database for later analysis. To ensure that the SQL Server database does not become too unwieldy, the data collected will be summarized on a regular basis and copied into summary tables in the database. As you would expect, once the data is in SQL Server, it can be consumed by a range of tools, including Microsoft Access and Excel.

9

SOAP, Web Services, and UDDI

Web services are starting to emerge as a key component of conducting business across the Internet.

A Web service is a piece of application logic that can provide some functionality to other applications connecting to it using Web-based protocols. Normally used in the context of Internet business-to-business, there is no reason why departments within a company could not use Web services to work together.

The precise implementation of a Web service is irrelevant, assuming it adheres to some agreed protocols and formats, freeing up organizations to be creative and perhaps start to convert existing applications into Web services. In fact, other Web service types often talk about e-services, dynamic services, and smart services—all of which fall under the same definition as our Web service (see Figure 9.1).

Web services can be linked to create a workflow application or maybe process a business transaction.

9.1   Simple Object Access Protocol (SOAP)

Out of all the acronyms that pervade the computing industry SOAP must be one of the most bizarre and a testament to the resourceful nature of the protocol inventors. That aside, SOAP is set to change the way in which applications are written for the Internet.

9.1.1   SOAP—A Historical Perspective

Before Microsoft discovered the Internet and did one of the smartest three-point turns in its history, the world of Microsoft distributed applications was very COM shaped. In fact, COM and its sister, distributed DCOM

Figure 9.1
*Typical Web
service.*

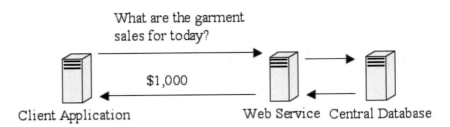

laid out a pretty compelling architecture used by many developers building
some fairly complex systems.

9.1.2 COM and DCOM

COM is a component software architecture, standardizing the way in
which objects interoperate. By providing a mechanism that allows objects
to communicate, developers can build applications using constituent elements from different vendors in the knowledge that the components should
interact to an agreed standard.

COM provides a component software architecture that is

■ Programming-language-independent

■ A binary standard for component interoperability

■ Extensible

It also allows applications to communicate across process and network
boundaries, share memory, and provide a mechanism to manage errors and
the dynamic loading of components.

COM is available on platforms other than Microsoft Windows, including Apple Macintosh and UNIX, but the main demand for COM applications is within Windows applications.

With the advent of the Internet, COM developers immediately tried to
apply COM mechanics on top of HTTP. It was soon evident that COM
was not Internet friendly and caused a number of problems, especially since
firewalls immediately stripped out any non-Internet protocols or procedure
calls, leaving nothing of use behind (see Figure 9.2).

An alternative had to be found that was language-neutral, was scalable,
and would gain broad support in the same way as other Internet protocols
such as HTTP.

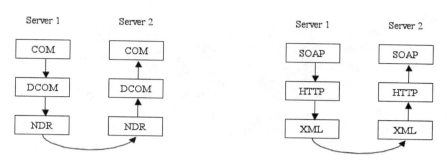

Figure 9.2
*Distributed
Applications—
DCOM versus
SOAP.*

So, along came SOAP.

Although very active in its promotion, Microsoft did not invent SOAP; the credit for the original work is spread among a number of engineers, including Don Box (now of Microsoft) and his Developmentor colleagues, IBM and Lotus. The original specification for SOAP was submitted to the Internet Engineering Task Force and announced publicly at a Microsoft conference in 2000.

SOAP is a protocol specification that defines a way of accessing or invoking remote services across HTTP, the standard Internet wire protocol. SOAP defines the structure and format of remote procedure calls and uses XML to represent the parameters and any returned values. Since SOAP is built on top of HTTP, it is firewall-friendly and has inherent scalability (see Figure 9.3).

It's important to remember that SOAP does not kill off COM; all it does is provide a way for objects to communicate across the Internet. What SOAP does do is compete head to head with DCOM and, in fact, will replace DCOM as the mechanism of choice for building distributed systems in any scenario other than dedicated corporate networks.

Due to its inherent simplicity, SOAP does have some downsides. By relying on XML to package data, large messages are often created—with associated performance costs. Neither does SOAP have an inherent security model or support for the more powerful RPC features found within such technologies as COM. This is the consequence of designing a simple, cross-platform protocol designed for mass acceptance.

The lack of a security model often worries IT professionals reviewing SOAP. Surely this is a huge flaw in the design of SOAP? No, not really. SOAP merely provides the transport mechanism; unless you have a service capable of receiving the incoming messages, they will just fall off the edge of the planet into obscurity. In addition, the standard SOAP headers allow

Figure 9.3
SOAP in action.

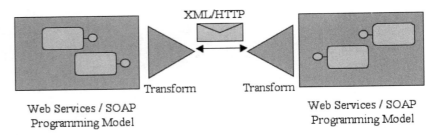

XML/HTTP

Transform   Transform

Web Services / SOAP   Web Services / SOAP
Programming Model   Programming Model

firewall administrators to turn off SOAP packets if they so wish. In fact, you would always put a security layer in your system and that would be HTTPS or SSL or any other standard security model, all of which work quite happily with SOAP.

One aspect of computing that is not addressed by SOAP is bidirectional communication. This does severely limit the use of SOAP for transactional usage, although there is an existing RFC transactional protocol called Transaction Internet Protocol (TIP) that is slowly gaining recognition and does add this functionality to the SOAP protocol.

9.2   SOAP, DIME, and Binary Data

So far we have seen that SOAP supports data from any XML schema, but what about binary data? The Direct Internet Message Encapsulation (DIME) specification defines a way of packaging up binary data into a SOAP message.

This is useful when confronted with the non-XML world, such as with electronic data interchange (EDI). Clearly, EDI documents can be converted to XML, and indeed BizTalk Server (see Chapter 4) has tools to do this precise transformation. The problem with the conversion process is that it will introduce an overhead since the data is serialized on one end and then deserialized at the other. If we only wanted to transfer the message, this would be rather time-consuming and inefficient, especially when the data has been compressed using some efficient binary compression algorithm. Another example would be images that could be converted to relatively large XML files, but why bother when you have a perfectly good JPEG or GIF image file?

Digital signing introduces further complexities. By its very nature, the binary data has been signed at origin, and if you interfere with the data to convert it into XML and back again for the SOAP message, the signature will be invalidated.

DIME is a mechanism that allows a SOAP message and an associated set of binary data to be transmitted as a single entity. A DIME message consists of one or more records, each with associated headers and data sections. The data in each of the records can vary in length, but the precise sequence of the records must be maintained. One of the benefits of DIME is that data can be "chunked," so that large amounts of data can be split into smaller segments for transmission, overcoming the limitations of some systems to cope with large data sets in one go.

9.3 Universal Description, Discovery, and Integration (UDDI)

UDDI is another delightful set of letters that forms part of the .NET acronym jungle. UDDI is not a Microsoft-owned initiative and is actually stronger due to the fact that a number of industry organizations are supporting the UDDI initiative as the way for a business to do the following:

- Describe its services

- Discover other businesses offering services

- Provide a framework to integrate into other businesses electronically

A good analogy is a typical set of telephone directories. In a number of countries there are three types of business directories: white pages of business contact information; yellow pages, which categorize businesses by agreed taxonomies; and green pages, which document the information about available services.

Imagine wading through thousands of businesses in white pages trying to determine whether the business is suitable to work with, and then have to decide the best way to interface with the technology a business may have in place. UDDI is designed to make the searching of online businesses and, once you have found your business partner, describing the best way to interface with its systems much easier.

UDDI is designed to reduce the cost of setting up a business-to-business environment and help integrate disparate business processes (see Figure 9.4).

UDDI is platform- and vendor-independent, enabling anyone to adopt this standard as a way to describe a business venture. In terms of the technology employed, UDDI is based on XML, SOAP, and HTTP and does

Figure 9.4
*UDDI network
with nodes
containing copies of
registered Web
service
information.*

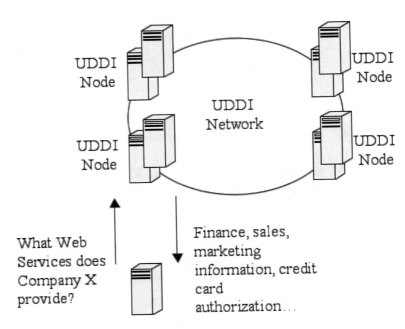

not introduce a new technology—rather, it suggests a standard way of using what we have. The companies behind UDDI (which include Microsoft, IBM, Oracle, SAP AG, and some other key players in the industry) have not set themselves up as another standards body—instead, they are actively working with W3C and IETF to ratify the UDDI initiative.

UDDI open draft version 1 was published on September 6, 2000, with two subsequent versions issued after nine-month periods before final standards submission.

UDDI Business Registry

The registry is the central hub of UDDI and provides the repository for information about businesses and services they provide. This, in turn, is used by those wishing to search for business partners. Any business can register, but the main purpose of UDDI is to assist businesses looking for Web services.

The UDDI business registry has not been designed to compete with any current business registries; instead, it will focus on providing a global, high-level repository, referring any detailed searches to local repositories.

The registry is currently run as a distributed service by IBM, Microsoft, and HP—all of which signed a service-level agreement to guarantee system availability; this is overseen by an operator's council, which polices the network.

Each "node operator," as they are called, runs a registry service containing a full and up-to-date listing of UDDI entries, with new entries being replicated to each node to ensure the systems are synchronized, in a manner similar to the Domain Name Service on the Internet, but on a (currently) much smaller scale. The replication of the services is through a set of common APIs agreed upon by the operator's council.

To achieve a listing on UDDI, a business must apply through a UDDI registrar, who will take the core business information and translate it into "UDDI speak" for the central repository.

There are four types of information stored in the registry:

1. **Business entity.** This contains the base information concerning a business. Each entity will have a unique identifier, the business name, a description of the business, contact information, a URL to the company's Web site, and a list of categories and identifiers describing the business it does.

2. **Business service.** Each business entity will have a list of services or things it can do. Each of these entries has a business description, a list of categories, and a list of pointers to references and information relating to the services.

3. **Specification pointers.** Each of the business service entries has a list of templates pointing to technical information about a particular service. Typically this would point to a URL, which, in turn, supplies information on how a service is invoked. The specification pointer will also link a service to a service type.

4. **Service type.** UDDI uses a tModel, which is metadata about a specification, to define a service type. Any number of businesses can offer the same type of service as defined in the tModel. The tModel will specify the information, such as the tModel name, publishing organization, message formats, message protocols, and security protocols.

Searching the registry is straightforward since it supports both a Web-based interface and an API. All of the taxonomies and classification schemes are based on industry standard categories, and a business can be searched on industry, product category, and geographical location.

9.4   The Web Service Interface

Specifications that describe a Web service interface are pointed to by a binding Template and a tModel. In fact, UDDI does not prescribe any technology or methodology to describe a Web interface since this can be described in a number of ways—such as simple prose or a formal description language. One of the common methods currently used to describe interfaces is Web Services Description Language (WSDL) or its sister, Web Services Conversation Language (WSCL). That said, there is no formal relationship between UDDI and these languages; they are just complementary.

9.5   UDDI XML Schema

The UDDI specifications contain both an XML schema for use by SOAP messages and a description of the UDDI API.

Within the XML schema there are four core types of information that provide everything a developer would need to know to utilize a partner's Web service.

1.   Business information

2.   Service information

3.   Binding information

4.   Specification information

9.5.1   Business Information Element

The chances are that organizations wishing to utilize your Web service will have some information about your company, such as the name, or a business identifier, such as a Dun and Bradstreet or company registration number. The businessEntity structure uses XML elements to store information about a business. The structure of the businessEntity element is such that yellow-pages-type searches can be conducted against a business to find out where the business is located or which specific industrial categories it serves.

9.5.2   Services Information Elements

The green-pages data, which has technical and business descriptions of the services provided, is stored in substructures of the businessEntity element.

These structures are the businessService and bindingTemplate. The businessService element stores a group of Web services that relate to a business process or set of services, as well as other technical information to describe the technical side of the services.

9.5.3 Binding and Specification Information

Knowing that a Web service sits on your business partner's Web site at a specific URL is only half the battle. There is a host of other information about the service, such as the security model used, the protocols used, and the format of the document, that needs to be known before you can start to connect to the service and exchange data. This information is called the Web service technical fingerprint and is stored in the bindingTemplate information element.

UDDI and Runtime Support

Runtime support is probably one of the most important issues to developers building UDDI-based solutions. The use of the business registry is fine for design-time activities, but developers building Web services need to be able to query UDDI programmatically.

Building reliable applications using Web services introduces a host of issues concerned with service-level agreements and intercompany support for applications. If a Web service should fail, how is the developer expected to manage the failure and allow alternate Web services to be used or to close down the application gracefully? On the other hand, the Web service provider needs to manage and maintain its own servers and needs to be able to inform service consumers of changes dynamically so that applications are not broken.

UDDI does have a role to play in providing a service-level guarantee to service providers and consumers. It has a calling convention, which caches binding information about the implementation that can be refreshed if a failure occurs.

The typical run-time process is as follows. The Web service is searched for within UDDI. Once discovered, the WSDL file and any implementation details are utilized from the UDDI bindingTemplate, which contains such things as the access point and configuration information. The client application needs to retrieve all of the relevant information from UDDI; it does this by caching the bindingKey of the Web service. The remote Web service is then invoked using the cached data from the UDDI Web registry.

If there is a problem running the Web service, two APIs—the bind-ingKey value and *get_bindingTemplate*—are called to refresh the binding information. The new and old information are then compared, and, if there is a difference, the failed call is retried so that the cached data can be refreshed for later use. If the binding information is the same, the Web service provider hasn't made any changes, and this will be detected by the application.

Almost inevitably the Web service will be updated, so if a redirection to a new Web service location needs to be made, the only change that needs to be made is the access point in the UDDI registry. All subsequent Web service access will then be to the new location—be it temporary or permanent.

Using UDDI Internally

The following example will give you an idea of how UDDI and Web services can be used in an organization. The example will focus on access to information regarding daily sales of garments from a private Web service deployed by the sales department of a clothing company.

The garment Web service is simple since it only has a single method, called *GetGarmentSales*, that allows access to a SQL Server database fed from a point-of-sale system from the store's network. This is updated using a BizTalk Server–based message queue infrastructure and is constantly refreshed with new incoming transactions. The client that wishes to access this sales information will cache the access point and bindingKey informa-tion and have some built-in robustness by refreshing its UDDI registry cache if there is a failure.

The Web service is built inside Visual Studio.NET using an appropriate .NET language, such as Visual Basic or C#. Since the Web service is fairly simple, it has a single method, *GetGarmentSales*, that retrieves garment sales based on two times given as input, so that garment sales can be seen from, for example, 10:00 A.M. to 3:00 P.M. The Web service code is created and then saved as an .asmx page called GetGarmentSales.asmx.

The page needs to be stored in a virtual directory on a Web site. To deploy the Web service it needs to be registered into an internal or private UDDI Server. Microsoft provides a local UDDI server in Microsoft Win-dows .NET Server, or developers can install a local UDDI server by using the Microsoft UDDI SDK.

The Web service can be registered via the Web user interface or directly using the UDDI SDK, which is probably the preferred method to speed up the process. The WSDL file needs to be registered as a tModel, which will

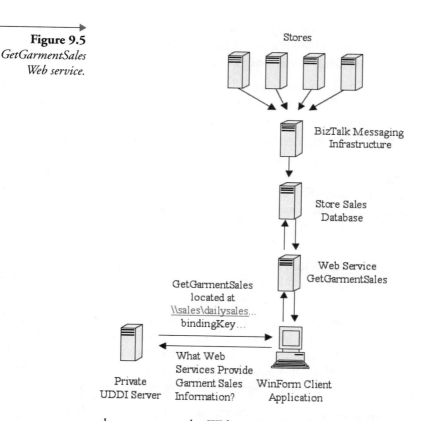

Figure 9.5
*GetGarmentSales
Web service.*

Stores

BizTalk Messaging
Infrastructure

Store Sales
Database

Web Service
GetGarmentSales

GetGarmentSales
located at
\\sales\dailysales...
bindingKey...

What Web
Services Provide
Garment Sales
Information?

Private
UDDI Server

WinForm Client
Application

then represent the Web service interfaces as XML and abstract any associated metadata. The access point for the Web service is then registered as a bindingTemplate, which is an XML-based structure used to show how a Web service has been implemented. The key values generated by UDDI are unique for our Web service entities and provide a way of identifying our service uniquely throughout UDDI (see Figure 9.5).

The accessPoint and bindingKey are two important bits of information used by the client to identify the correct Web service and then use the accessPoint to find the URL and location of the service. If at any time the client needs access to the WSDL, the tModelKey is used to query UDDI to return it.

9.6 Consuming an Internal Web Service

When designing the client, our garment Web service would be "discovered" by developers wishing to utilize it. The WSDL file would be downloaded and a proxy class generated using Add Web Reference in Visual Studio.NET or a command-line tool called WSDL.exe, which ships as part of the Microsoft .NET Framework SDK. In practice, most developers would probably be using Visual Studio.

The utilization application in our example will be a Windows Form application (Win Form standalone executable) used by users to query the sales figures.

The UDDI .NET SDK classes need to be added to the project and then a configuration file built to store the access point for the UDDI server that located our garment sales Web service since UDDI also runs as a Web service. The bindingKey of the Web service is also stored in the same configuration file, which, as expected, will exist as an XML file. The configuration file will be stored in the /bin directory once the application is compiled or built and will then be named after the executable file.

The client application is now built with all of the usual buttons and text boxes, which will enable the sales search parameters to be entered into the form as users search for sales across a certain time period.

Application code is added as you would expect, but we add an additional function to query the UDDI server to find the Web service access point. The actual accessPoint value is stored as a variable, so if the application is restarted, UDDI will be requeried for the accessPoint value, enabling any changes to the Web service to be automatically refreshed.

If there is a problem with accessing the service, the application will automatically try to check out the status of the Web service.

If the accessPoint is requeried and the same value is returned, it is a good indicator that the service provider has not updated the service and there is probably a problem with the service at that moment in time. At that point there is not a lot an application can do other than let the service provider know its Web service is broken!

If a different value for accessPoint is returned from UDDI, the Web service can be invoked again since it has probably been updated by the service provider.

9.7   .NET MyServices

Originally codenamed "Hailstorm," Microsoft .NET MyServices are a proposed range of XML-based consumer services designed to make the management and dissemination of personal information easy but secure.

Figure 9.6 *.NET MyServices in action.*

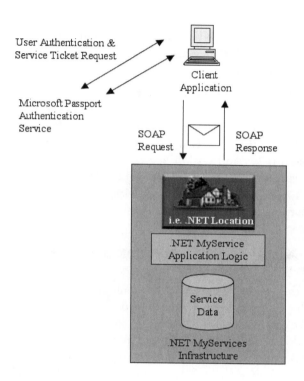

Microsoft has gained considerable experience in running large Web-based services, such as Hotmail and the Microsoft Passport authentication site. It was apparent that there was a possible business model in extending these services to cover other areas, which, in turn, could become a revenue opportunity for the organization. At the time of writing, Microsoft has defocused its efforts around .NET MyServices while it reevaluates the proposed business model. The underlying technology still stands and acts as an example of how Web services will start to revolutionize development and deployment across the Web.

How .NET MyServices Will Work

It's no surprise to find out that .NET MyServices will be a collection of XML-based Web services accessed by sending and receiving SOAP messages through HTTP or DIME using Microsoft Passport as the authentication service (see Figure 9.6).

Web sites that use .NET Passport sign-in services have what is called a scarab on their site page that users click onto and then enter their Passport sign-in name and password. The hosting site then initiates a request to the

Passport site for a ticket granting ticket (TGT). If the password and sign-in name are correct, .NET Passport will grant the TGT, which, in turn, indicates to users that they have successfully signed in. The TGT will be cached for later use.

The TGT is then presented to .NET Passport, which is now acting as a ticket granting server (TGS), and a session ticket is requested for the appropriate .NET MyServices being used. .NET Passport will use the TGT to verify who the client is and that the client has not expired; then, it returns a session ticket and session key to .NET MyServices. All of the encryption between the client and service will now be encrypted using this session key. Access to the various services within .NET MyServices will be granted according to the session ticket.

9.8 Global XML Web Services Architecture (GXA)

As the various Web service technologies gain hold, there are a number of holes in the current standards as different organizations innovate and produce new solutions. To bridge this ever-expanding gap, Microsoft has worked with IBM to design an architectural sketch to fill in a number of areas, including security, routing, reliable messaging, and transactions. This architecture, called GXA, was presented to a World Wide Web Consortium workshop in April 2001. The specifications within GXA represent what is called a composable architecture, in that the suggested specifications are used alongside other specifications already accepted within the standards body.

The design of GXA is based on some fundamental themes:

- GXA is designed for broad coverage of a range of Web services solutions, including business-to-business, enterprise application integration, and business-to-consumer.

- GXA employs a modular approach, so that features can be employed when needed but without the overhead of carrying unneeded functionality. In addition, when new features are developed they can be added as required.

- GXA does not need a centralized server or administration since it is a federated service. It is technology-independent and does not need specific implementation technology at the message end points.

- GXA is based on standards such as SOAP, WSDL, and UDDI and Microsoft is proposing to keep GXA in the realm of industry standards.

9.8.1 GXA Security

Undoubtedly, security is one of the most important aspects of Internet commerce. With the impending proliferation of Web services, by definition, heterogeneous systems will be connecting using a range of technologies and implementations that will need to trust each other—or the concept of Web services will collapse.

WS-Security describes the process of using the standard W3C security specifications, XML Signature and XML Encryption, to ensure that SOAP messages are secure. WS-Security is a straightforward, stateless extension to SOAP that explains how credentials are placed within SOAP messages.

WS-License is a mechanism that uses existing license formats, such as X.509 and Kerberos tickets, as WS-Security credentials. Its extensibility model is designed to accommodate new license formats as they become incorporated into the specification.

9.8.2 GXA Routing

The variety of communication technologies in use on the Internet means that SOAP messages need to be transmitted across a number of technical boundaries. WS-Routing and WS-Referral support this.

WS-Routing is a stateless extension for SOAP that allows messages to be sent asynchronously over a range of communication transports, including TCP, UDP, and HTTP. It also includes a mechanism for two-way messaging.

WS-Referral allows a SOAP node to pass on its processing responsibility to another SOAP node.

9.8.3 Reliable Messaging

Transmission errors are part and parcel of the Internet due to its complex nature. For commerce to succeed in this environment it is critical that messages sent from one place to another arrive on time and intact. This protocol provides a guarantee of delivery with an easy-to-use error-handling model, so that developers are not buried in the detail of messaging semantics. There are built-in messaging guarantees, so that end-to-end delivery is ensured and messages are not lost or duplicated.

9.8.4 Transaction Management

Transactions—atomic units of work—are difficult to manage in a stateful networking environment. Couple transactions with the stateless Internet, and problems will occur. In many situations, a far looser transaction model is preferred and will still enable the business to be effective. GXA provides the architecture for building and deploying transaction models across the Internet.

Scalability and Security

Without a doubt, Microsoft has undergone a huge change in attitude toward security following an announcement in 2001 that all product feature development would cease for six months while the product groups reviewed the security aspects of their products.

Scalability has always been an issue for Microsoft, as they start to penetrate enterprise-level applications. The ability for the software to grow inline with business requirements is one of the first issues raised by corporate IT departments. Windows NT was introduced a few years ago with the objective of providing the first scalable platform from Microsoft. Over the years, the platform has inevitably been enhanced, and with Windows 2000 we see a scalable enterprise operating system from Microsoft.

10.1 .NET Security

As you would expect, .NET comes with a lot of security built into the underlying framework. The security in .NET is based upon the concept of managed code, with the security of the code being looked after by the (CLR see Chapter 3). Managed code is checked to ensure that it is type-safe, so that incorrectly calling a method declared as accepting an 8-byte value will reject a call from anything larger as not being type safe. This verification process also ensures that code executes using flow transfers to method entry points or other well-known locations rather than some random location.

The CLR does allow unmanaged code to run, but it will not manage any of the security of the application, and specific permissions need to be granted to allow calls to unmanaged code. Microsoft believes that .NET managed code will soon become the norm as the benefits become realized by developers and the incidence of unmanaged code decreases over time.

10.1.1   **Role-Based Security**

This is the model used by .NET to authorize and authenticate users. It uses the idea of a principal, who is the user on whose behalf code is run. The security model is also responsible for the authentication of the user name/password pair submitted by a principal.

A principal may be a member of a group of users that have a set of activities they are authorized to do, and these roles are examined when a user attempts to undertake a privileged operation. Roles include backups, adding new users, and accessing specific directories.

10.1.2   **Evidence-Based Security and Managed Code**

It's all very well trusting users, but what happens if Mrs. Miggins brings in a floppy disk from home with some code on it written by her son. Trusting code and restrictions on how code is executed are a basic part of how .NET is structured to ensure that rogue code does not trample over a user's machine, causing damage. Managed code—that is, code running within the .NET framework—can be limited to using well-defined interfaces. Applications can be built that run a host of components in the knowledge that security can be enforced at differing levels, according to the nature of the application. All of this code can run in-proces; the code permits previously risky scenarios, such as code for mobile devices, to be downloaded from insecure servers and executed safely, knowing that the code is subject to restrictions.

For managed code to run, a security policy will assess which permissions to grant based upon evidence from the code assembly and any specific requests from the code itself. The collection of evidence can be from a number of sources, including the site URL, the zone the code is from, or the existence of valid digital signatures.

Other evidence sources include the following:

- The hash value of an assembly generated with hash algorithms.

- The strong name signature of an assembly. Strong names represent a versioned, cryptographically strong way to refer to and identify an assembly or all assemblies of a particular signing party. They do not provide any authentication of the author, but they uniquely identify the assembly and ensure that it has not been tampered with.

- The site from which the code came. Assemblies are the building blocks of .NET framework applications. They form the fundamental unit of deployment, version control, reuse, activation scoping, and security authorization. An application's assemblies are downloaded to the client from a Web site.

■

- ■ The directory from which the code is loaded.
- ■ The Authenticode digital signature of the assembly.

If the code attempts to perform a function outside of the scope of its approved security rating, then quite simply the code won't run. Code can be examined at deployment time to see what permissions are required for it to run successfully.

In reality, most code that a developer writes would not need to use the evidence-based security explicitly, since that is looked after by the standard class libraries within the application. Whether or not the security model is used explicitly, developers can be assured that it is there anyway and that the entire application runs in the context of the evidence-based security model.

10.2 .NET Isolated Storage

Isolated storage is a useful feature of .NET that allows a segregated area to be created for storing data for an application even if no file access has been allowed. This is useful, for example, when a managed control is downloaded from the Internet. The control can be given a very limited set of permissions, but is prevented from reading or writing files. This area is only available to the specific assembly for which it was created. Typical use for this area would be to save settings or state information that needs to be persisted to disk for later use.

10.3 Declarative and Imperative Security

If a programmer specifies security requirements directly inside an assembly's metadata, he or she is implementing what is known as declarative security. All of the security settings are specified as customized attributes in the code and classes; methods and properties are used to fine-tune these permissions. A typical use of declarative security would be if a method needed to have write access to a specific disk location since the permissions and required actions will be known when the assembly is compiled.

Alternatively, imperative security would be used if the location of the write access changes. Imperative security is when the security is implemented within the code. All security tasks are undertaken programmatically, and appropriate rights are granted or denied based upon the security stack state.

10.4 Cryptography and .NET

The .NET framework has a number of cryptography functions that allow for encryption, digital signatures, hashing, and the generation of random numbers. The asymmetric algorithms, RSA and DSA, the symmetric algorithms, DES, TripleDES, and RC2, and the hashes, MD5 and SHA1, are all supported. These are implemented as stream-based algorithms so that data is streamed through the encryption function before being routed to a network location.

10.5 Digital Signatures

Digital certificates are electronic versions of identity cards or passports, and the issuing process is similar. An approved body, called the certification authority, checks information about a developer and, when it is satisfied, will issue a digital certificate. This will contain information about the developer and the certification authority that issued the certificate. So who certifies the certification authority? Well, there is a hierarchy of authorities, often starting from a government level, that ensures that only trusted bodies are approved to issue certificates. Hierarchical information is often included as part of the certificate, again, endorsing its authority.

Digital certificates are used to sign code, documents, and controls so that the source of these items can instantly be verified and displayed to a user to establish a trust relationship.

Certificate integrity is ensured by standard technology called public-key cryptography. This uses a matched pair of keys called a private key and a public key.

Keys use a large value, which makes it unfeasible for existing technology to break a key using brute computational effort. Note the careful use of the word *existing* since never is a long time and previous unbreakable keys have been hacked following recent advances in computing power!

To reduce the chances of a hacker deriving a private key from its associated public key, the certificate authority will timestamp a key pair so that the keys will need to be replaced on a regular basis. Signatures applied while a certificate is active will last ad infinitum, but those applied after a certificate expires will be invalid.

10.6 Scalability

There is a lot of confusion about scalability and application performance and many people confuse the two issues.

I have worked on many applications that were extremely fast. They performed exceptionally well, and the user was very happy that he or she could process so many widgets per hour so quickly using this wonderful new software. Then the business started to grow and more people were hired to work on the system; very soon the widget processing rate started to tumble since the solution could not scale to cope with more than five users.

Scalability has been brought into the spotlight with the advent of the Internet as a mainstream business tool. Alongside security, it must rate as one of the most important issues for Web site designers, and with the average user only being prepared to wait 20 seconds for a page to load, the implications for a poorly scaling site can be huge.

.NET is now introducing the idea of Web services (see Chapter 9) as a way to develop and deliver megaservices—that is, Web-based services designed to run 24x7 with no downtime. Alongside these services there is a whole new industry being developed for lawyers to write onerous service-level agreement contracts that guarantee a level of performance (really scalability) from each of these services. I guess, quite rightly, that your business can be at risk if an important Web service your customers use should fail through no fault of your own.

Scale up or Scale out

Microsoft has the benefit of hedging its bets on scalability, offering both a scale-out and a scale-up solution.

- **Scale up.** This is the solution that vendors of huge servers really enjoy. It basically means installing and configuring the largest possible multiprocessor server you can find and cramming it full of huge amounts of memory. The advantage is that you only have one box to manage, but the disadvantage is that you have one point of failure, and it is possibly very costly.

- **Scale out**. This appeals to PC enthusiasts since it uses commodity PC servers but networks them together to provide a large virtual server. The downside of scaling out is the need to have a set of management tools capable of running such a configuration, but the upside is that you can easily add additional hardware or, if the going gets tough, take hardware away!

10.7 NLB

NLB from Microsoft is a software solution—it doesn't need any special hardware to make it work. It comes as part of Windows 2000 Server, Advanced Server, and Datacenter Server. Microsoft Application Center is used to manage these NLB features using its centralized management interface. See Chapter 8 for further coverage of Application Center Server and load balancing.

10.7.1 CLB

CLB allows COM+ components to be load-balanced, reducing the potential bottleneck of the business component layer. More complex applications can sometimes make a lot of use of the component layer, which results in a huge demand for component resources; if they are physically located on the Web server, scalability of the Web site would be dramatically reduced. With CLB the components can also be installed on a separate physical server, which can be optimized with CLB and lots of memory.

As with NLB, CLB has been around since the early beta days of Windows 2000. It soon became apparent that it was a good idea, but poorly executed since the management of the components was complex. Application Center Server can also be used to manage component load balancing, as well as network load balancing. It also removes the possible single point of failure inherent in earlier designs.

How CLB Works

In essence, CLB distributes COM+ activations using a list of potential servers and their recorded response times. The servers are clustered together; this is known as the Web-tier cluster. A table of response times (the routing list) is dynamically updated every 200 ms, with the fastest responding server placed at the top and the others ranked under it. The routing list is copied to each server in the Web-tier cluster, so if a server fails, the routing list is

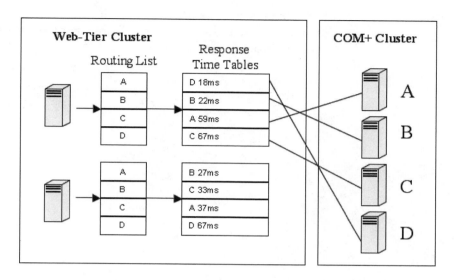

Figure 10.1
CLB, routing tables, and the COM+ cluster.

still available and CLB distribution continues as normal. This removes any likely single point of failure (see Figure 10.1).

The good news for the programmer is that no code changes are needed to make use of CLB, and once it is set up, it should just work and be transparent to users and developers alike (see Figure 10.2).

When Not To Use CLB

It must be said that there are times when using CLB will adversely affect the performance of your application—strange as it may seem. By using CLB you are calling across multiple servers across a network configuration. This will, by definition, incur a cost, due to the bandwidth of the network. If

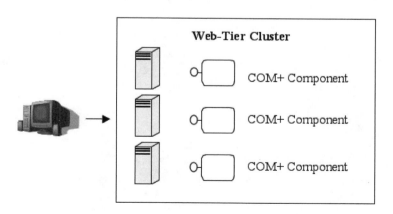

Figure 10.2
Installing the components directly on the Web-tier cluster.

throughput is essential for your site, Microsoft recommends that the components be installed locally on the Web-tier servers and that you do away with the separate component servers.

Microsoft SharePoint Portal Server

One of the more strangely named Microsoft .NET Enterprise Server products, but nevertheless one that is gaining a lot of attention, is SharePoint Portal Server. Designed originally by the Microsoft Office group as a departmental information sharing/finding and organizing solution, its appeal is fairly widespread since it provides a way of storing and searching large amounts of business data and documents.

11.1 The Portal

Portals are fast becoming the standard way of collecting information from different sources and then presenting it to users in a unified corporate manner across an intranet.

SharePoint Portal Server creates a Web portal or dashboard during installation. This provides a central access point for finding and managing documents and information. Users will interface with the portal via a Web browser such as Internet Explorer and will typically:

- Search for information
- Subscribe to new or updated information
- Browse through information sorted by categories
- Check documents in and out
- Review document's version histories
- Approve documents for publication
- Publish documents

The portal or dashboard is fully customizable so that an organization can tailor it to its specific look and feel, adding information feeds that may be important for its market sector. Figure 11.1 illustrates a typical portal.

Microsoft Digital Dashboard technology is used to organize and display information. This consists of a digital dashboard with reusable and customizable Web Parts that can present information from a wide variety of sources, including Microsoft Office documents and Web sites.

In addition, you can allow users to create customized "personal" dashboards to organize and present information that is especially relevant to them. This could be project- or department-related information such as a sales group or marketing team. Web Parts can be created directly from Office XP or by importing Web Parts from a centralized catalog (see Figure 11.2).

11.2 Management and Publishing of Documents

Anyone who has tried to manage documents using file shares soon realizes that it is near to impossible, and even if it is achievable it requires a lot of manual intervention as files are copied from one location to another. The main problem is that there is only one navigation path to any given document, and users must know the name of the server that the document is stored on, in addition to the directory structure of folders on the server. When you add other sources of information, such as Web sites, e-mail serv-

Figure 11.1 *A typical portal.*

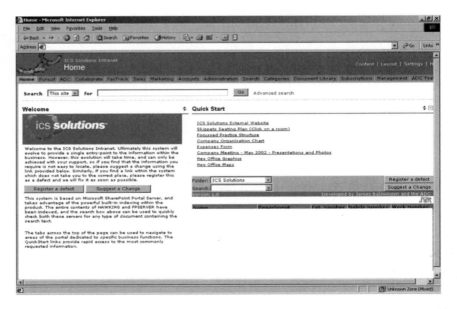

Figure 11.2
The Web Parts catalog allows users to customize their portals.

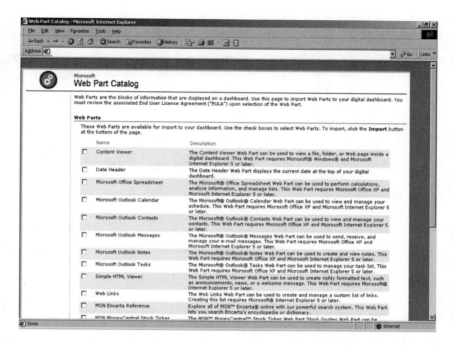

ers, and databases to the mix of information sources, finding the right information can be almost impossible. As an aside, "Longhorn," the version of Windows planned for release after Windows .NET Server, is rumored to be heavily focused on helping users find their documents and files—this being a passionate goal of Bill Gates. I am sure many millions of frustrated Windows users share the same passions!

SharePoint Portal Server (SPPS) offers a number of features to help users manage documents and files (see Figure 11.3).

- Document publishing control

- Version tracking to record the history of documents as they are edited

- Application of metadata to identify a document

- Automated approval routes for documents to be sent to other users for review

- Web discussions for online comments by multiple document users or reviewers

Figure 11.3
*SharePoint Portal
Server—Managing
the users and
creating personal
dashboards.*

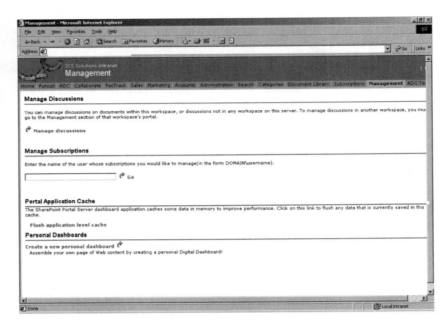

11.3   SharePoint Portal Server Category Assistant

Categories can be used to efficiently sort files and information. For example, a sales category containing sales-related information would be a starting point for a new sales-person. The problem is that with a large number of documents, categorizing them can be a time-consuming task. To simplify the process, SharePoint Portal Server provides an automated categorization tool called the Category Assistant. After a few representative documents have been categorized for each category, the Category Assistant compares those sample documents to the uncategorized documents and then automatically selects the best category matches based on the content in the uncategorized documents. This is a very smart piece of technology based on some smart-ranking algorithms from Microsoft Research (see Figure 11.4).

11.4   SharePoint Portal Server Version Control

A document's history is recorded by SharePoint Portal Server to help track changes and eliminate the possibility of someone overwriting another user's modifications. Before a document is edited it needs to be checked out of SharePoint Portal Server, preventing others from changing it until it is checked back in. When a document is checked back in SharePoint Portal

Server assigns a new version number and the previous version is archived. When documents are checked out, the most recent version is retrieved unless the user specifically selects an earlier version.

11.5 **SharePoint Portal Server Document Publishing**

SharePoint Portal Server can store both "private" and "public" versions of a document. Documents are automatically published each time documents are checked in, but if need be they can be checked in as private drafts and only published when the document is complete. Multiple drafts can be completed before publishing a version of a document. Only published documents are available for users to search or view on a dashboard site (see Figure 11.5).

11.5.1 **Document Profiles**

Document profiles provide a way to add searchable information (metadata) to a document. By default, a document profile includes basic properties such as author and title but custom metadata can be requested to capture additional information that makes it easier to organize and find documents.

Figure 11.4
Categories in SharePoint Portal Server.

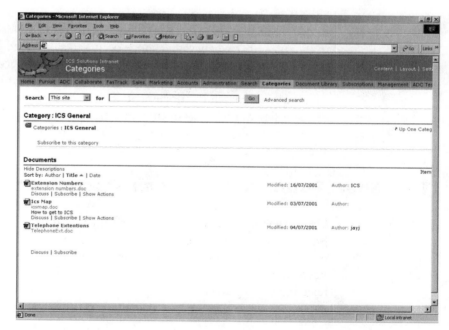

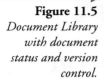

Figure 11.5
Document Library
with document
status and version
control.

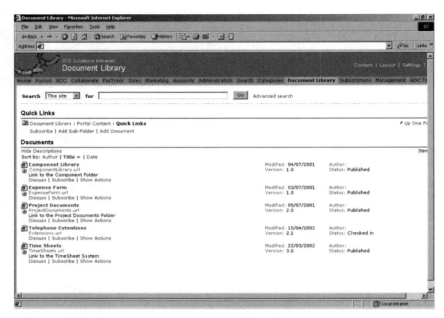

11.5.2   Subscriptions

SharePoint Portal Server subscriptions enable users to subscribe to changes in documents, folders, categories, and search results. Notifications are sent to the subscriber whenever a change occurs to subscribed objects. Subscriptions are implemented by using Persistent Query Service (PQS) rules, which evaluate a large set of queries against a single document to determine which queries match the document. This allows matching subscriptions to be identified as each new document arrives in the SharePoint Portal Server store. Subscriptions provide the "push" model to match the "pull" model of a full-text search.

11.6   SharePoint Portal Server Document Approval

Once a document has been created, it may need to be adequately reviewed prior to publication. When an author chooses to publish a document, it can be sent automatically to one or more people for review before publishing. Each of these people, called approvers, has the option of approving or rejecting the document.

This process is facilitated by e-mail, and approvers will receive e-mail notification when a document requires review. SharePoint Portal Server

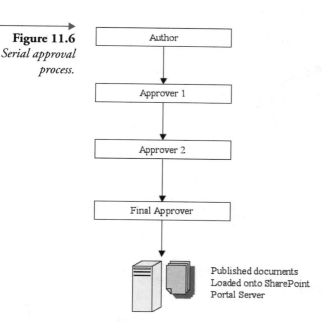

Figure 11.6
*Serial approval
process.*

supports two approval routes: serial and parallel (see Figure 11.6 through 11.8).

11.7 SharePoint Portal Server Security

SharePoint Portal Server uses roles to control access to content. Users are assigned the coordinator, author, and reader roles, depending upon their jobs within an organization.

Figure 11.7
*Parallel single—
Any one approver
can authorize the
document.*

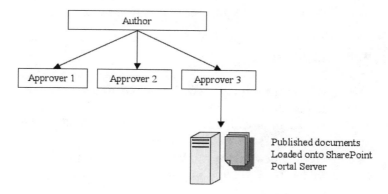

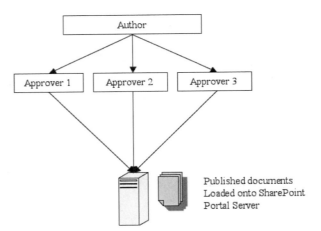

Figure 11.8
Parallel all—All approvers must authorize the document.

11.7.1 Coordinator

A coordinator manages content in the top-level folder and performs a set of workspace administration tasks, including managing content sources, document profiles, categories, and subscriptions, and customizing the dashboard site. The coordinator also creates indexes of updated content when necessary or schedules this to occur automatically.

A coordinator on a specific folder configures user roles on the folder. The coordinator creates subfolders and adds, edits, and deletes documents from them. Coordinators can also read and delete a document that has been created but is not yet checked in. For enhanced folders, the coordinator selects the appropriate approval process. In addition, the coordinator can undo the check-out of a document or end the publishing process by using the Cancel Publishing or Bypass Approval actions.

11.7.2 Author

An author can add new documents to a folder, edit all documents in the folder, delete any document from the folder, and read all documents in the folder. In an enhanced folder, authors can also submit any document for publishing. An author can create, rename, and delete folders. When you create a new folder, it inherits the roles and folder policies from the parent folder. However, the author cannot change the roles or the approval policy on folders he or she creates.

11.7.3   Reader

A reader can search for and read documents but cannot add them to the workspace. By default, all folder users have read permissions. In an enhanced folder, readers can view only folders and published versions of documents. Enhanced folders provide increased document management functions, including approval routing and version control. A reader cannot check out, edit, or delete workspace documents and cannot view draft document versions.

By default, SharePoint Portal Server assigns the Windows 2000 Everyone group to the reader role for all folders in the workspace when it creates the workspace.

SharePoint Portal Server also offers the option of denying a user access to specific files or documents.

Discussing a document without modifying its content can be time consuming. SharePoint Portal Server uses Web discussions, which allow simultaneous discussions between reviewers and authors. Comments are stored as threaded conversations, grouping comments and replies together. With all comments grouped into a single place, document authors no longer need to compile hand-written comments from reviewers or comments sent through individual e-mail messages.

11.8   SPPS Indexing and Searching Technologies

SharePoint Portal Server has a set of fairly advanced search and retrieval technologies. SharePoint Portal Server uses protocol handlers and a gatherer to crawl and provide search over data from a variety of different content sources.

SharePoint Portal Server can crawl documents stored on:

- File systems
- Web sites
- Exchange 2000 Server and Exchange Server 5.5 computers
- Lotus Notes servers
- Other SharePoint Portal Server workspaces

SharePoint Portal Server is not designed to provide access to conventional relational databases, but it is possible to crawl database information if you can access the database using HTTP and build an ASP page to render the data. Document locations that are not covered by SharePoint Portal Server natively may be accessed by writing specific protocol handlers for those location types using the SharePoint Portal Server software development kit (SDK).

SharePoint Portal Server indexing uses language-specific word breakers and stemmers to extract words from the content. These "noise" words (e.g., a, the, of) are filtered out, and the content index is generated. Specific-language support is provided for English, French, Spanish, Italian, German, Traditional Chinese, Simplified Chinese, Korean, Thai, Dutch, Swedish, and Japanese. A "neutral" word breaker is used for all other languages.

11.9 SharePoint Portal Server Filters

Filters are used to reach specific file format types. Natively SharePoint Portal Server includes filters for:

- Microsoft Office documents
- HTML files
- Tagged Image File Format (TIFF) files
- Text files

The TIFF filter enables SharePoint Portal Server to crawl the textual content of saved fax data based on Optical Character Recognition (OCR) technology. SharePoint Portal Server uses the Multipurpose Internet Mail Extensions (MIME) filter that ships with Windows 2000 when filtering messages from Exchange public folders.

SharePoint Portal Server also supports third-party and custom file types, such as the Adobe PDF filter, and a number of vendors are providing filters for their file formats.

SharePoint Portal Server uses SQL full-text extensions. Queries are submitted using Distributed Authoring and Versioning Searching and Locating (DASL) requests—part of HTTPDAV, which is HTTP Document Authoring and Versioning.

11.10 SPPS Search Ranking

SharePoint Portal Server offers an advanced ranking algorithm, based on work undertaken by Microsoft Research. This algorithm ensures that the documents most relevant to a user's query are returned at the top of the list of search results, based upon a probabilistic ranking of searched material.

The ranking of a document is based upon a number of factors, including:

- Document length
- Frequency of the query term in the entire collection of documents
- Number of documents in the entire collection of documents
- Number of documents containing the query term

To force certain documents or files to appear higher up a ranking, Best Bets can be used. This feature enables users with appropriate permissions to tag individual documents as most appropriate for specific queries or categories. Even in the most advanced probabilistic ranking environment, certain documents lack the textual information to be prominent in search results for particular terms.

The Best Bets feature addresses this problem, either by advancing the specially tagged documents to the top of the results list or by displaying them prominently when browsing categories. The SharePoint Portal Server dashboard site also nominates Best Bet documents when the rank of the document is very high.

11.10.1 Automatic Categorization and Schema Support

In addition to simple search, SharePoint Portal Server provides automatic categorization. This feature enables the user to define a category hierarchy and then use a sample set of documents within the hierarchy as a training sample. After training, documents stored on the server and crawled documents are automatically tagged and appear in the category hierarchy.

SharePoint Portal Server provides simplified schema management facilities, which are Office compatible through the use of promotion and demotion. Users define document profiles and associated properties. During promotion, property values in the Office document are copied to the properties of a SharePoint Portal Server document profile. During demotion, property values found in a SharePoint Portal Server document profile are copied to the Office document. Full-text search in SharePoint Portal Server is tightly integrated with that schema. Advanced search uses properties and document profiles.

11.11 SharePoint Portal Server and Adaptive Crawling

Microsoft introduced incremental crawling with Site Server 3.0, which uses time-stamp comparisons to include only documents that have changed since the previous update of the index.

Incremental updates reduce the amount of indexing work involved in repeated crawls but do not eliminate the need to inspect the time stamp of each document previously crawled each time a crawl occurs. Adaptive crawling goes one step further. During crawls, the algorithm for adaptive crawling gathers statistics about the rate of change for each document. In subsequent adaptive crawls, the algorithm targets only documents that are likely to have changed.

11.12 SharePoint Portal Server Architecture

SharePoint Portal Server integrates with a number of key Microsoft technologies, including Windows, Office, Digital Dashboards, Microsoft Internet Explorer, the Microsoft Exchange Server Web Storage System, and Microsoft Search Service. Each of these technologies has been around for a while, but Microsoft has tapped into each of them to build the features of SharePoint Portal Server (see Figure 11.9).

The client components allow users to perform document management and search tasks and consist of extensions to Office applications and Windows Explorer. The browser-based dashboard site provides a Web-based view on the document management and search services in SharePoint Portal Server. The core server components include Document Management Services, Search Services, and the Digital Dashboard and Web Parts Runtime environment.

11.13 SharePoint Portal Server Scalability

Originally SharePoint Portal Server was designed for building and deploying workgroup-based solutions. It is now being used in a number of large

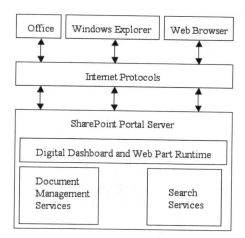

Figure 11.9
SharePoint Portal Server architecture.

intranet installations, and Microsoft has made available a license for using SharePoint Portal Server across the Internet.

So how scalable is it? SharePoint Portal Server is scalable enough to handle:

- More than 500,000 documents stored in a single server, single document management workspace

- More than 500,000 documents using a similar single server configuration where a majority of the content is stored on external information stores

- More than 1,000,000 documents when dedicated SharePoint Portal Server content index and search server configurations are used to index external content stores

11.13.1   SharePoint Portal Server Solution Architecture

Due to its scalability SharePoint Portal Server can be deployed in a number of different ways, depending on the organizational requirements.

Example 1—Departmental team with Single SharePoint Portal Server

The first example is a departmental team with a single SharePoint Portal Server computer with a workspace that consists almost entirely of content stored locally. The amount of content stored outside the workspace is small

Figure 11.10
Small departmental solution.

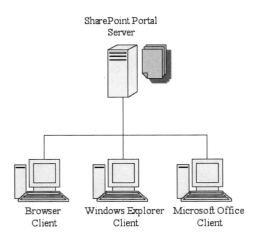

and might consist of content sources pointing to one or two competitors' Web sites. The emphasis is on the document management capabilities of SharePoint Portal Server rather than its search capabilities (see Figure 11.10).

Example 2—Search Services with Single SharePoint Portal Server

This second example is a team using SharePoint Portal Server to search content stored on its file servers, database servers, and an Internet Web site (see Figure 11.11). The dashboard site displays organization-wide communication, such as announcements, vacation schedules, and finance information. The SharePoint Portal Server computer stores indexes for the configured content sources and makes them available to the dashboard site associated with

Figure 11.11
Search Services with Single SharePoint Portal Server.

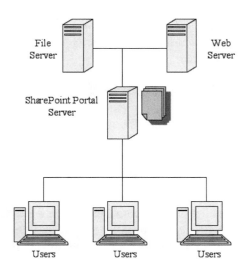

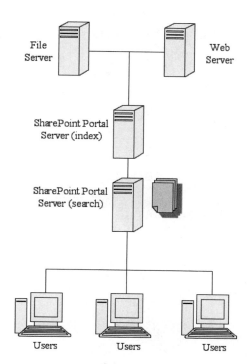

Figure 11.12
Multiple
SharePoint Portal
Server covering
different tasks in a
larger installation.

the workspace. In addition to the content sources that link to documents stored outside the workspace, the workspace itself can contain documents. The group primarily searches its own content, with limited searching on Internet sites. Document management is required only for the documents stored in the workspace. The only users performing document management tasks are those responsible for updating the dashboard site.

Example 3—Document Management and Aggregated Searches

For improved throughput in larger SharePoint Portal Server installations, multiple servers can be deployed—each of which performs a dedicated task, such as dedicated index server, and another server dedicated for front-end searching and providing the dashboard (see Figure 11.12).

Example 4—Organization-Wide Document Management and Searching

For very large organization-wide installations multiple servers are required to share the work load as efficiently as possible. This deployment will include at least three SharePoint Portal Server computers:

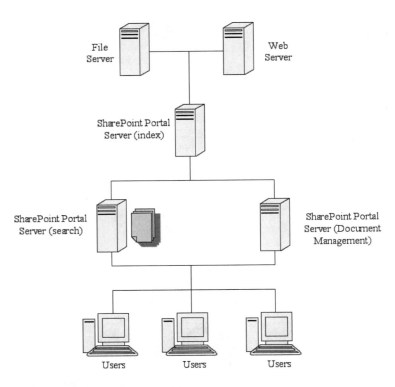

Figure 11.13
*Large-scale,
organization-wide
installation.*

- Server dedicated to searching
- Server dedicated to indexing
- One or more document management servers

The number of document management servers will depend on the number of users requiring that functionality and the volume of documents. Often, the allocation of servers will be per department, which also makes the associated management easier (see Figures 11.13 and 11.14).

11.14 Exchange 2000 Server and SharePoint Portal Server

SharePoint Portal Server can be installed on a server running Exchange 2000 Service Pack 1 or later. Exchange Server must be installed before installing SharePoint Portal Server, and Exchange Server does not install if the Microsoft Web Storage System already exists on the server. SharePoint Portal Server will upgrade the existing Microsoft Search service and the full-

Figure 11.14
Organizational use of SharePoint can improve project collaboration.

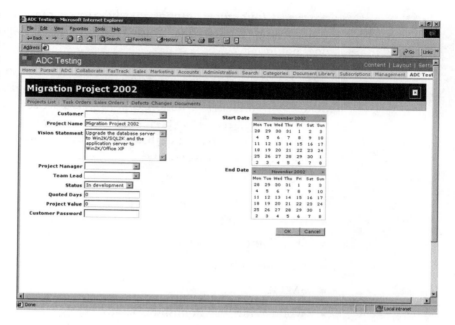

text index format of all the existing indexes on that computer the next time MSSearch starts. There must be enough disk space on the server to accommodate 120 percent of the size of the largest full-text index on the drive. Upgrading the full-text index format can take several hours, depending on the number and size of the existing indexes. During the SharePoint Portal Server setup, a message informs you that the service will be upgraded.

Additionally, since SharePoint Portal Server upgrades MSSearch and full-text indexes, SharePoint Portal Server must not be installed on a server that participates in an Exchange Server clustering environment, nor should a computer running SharePoint Portal Server be added to a clustered environment.

If you remove SharePoint Portal Server from a computer that has Exchange Server installed, the upgraded MSSearch is not removed, because it is a shared service with Exchange Server.

When you install SharePoint Portal Server on a computer running Exchange Server, SharePoint Portal Server stops the Microsoft Exchange Information Store (MSExchangeIS) service for a short time period. This results in a disruption of mail services during installation of SharePoint Portal Server.

Only four storage groups can exist on an Exchange Server computer. SharePoint Portal Server creates a new storage group during the installation process. If four storage groups already exist on the Exchange server when you attempt to install SharePoint Portal Server, SharePoint Portal Server does not install.

Exchange 2000 Server and SharePoint Portal Server share services. If you remove Exchange 2000 Server after you install SharePoint Portal Server, SharePoint Portal Server no longer works, because services formerly shared with Exchange Server have been modified. Even if you attempt to uninstall Exchange 2000 Server and then cancel the removal, SharePoint Portal Server may no longer work. In this case, you must manually restart the following services:

- IIS Admin Service
- SharePoint Portal Server
- Exchange Information Store
- SMTP
- World Wide Web Publishing Service
- Network News Transport Protocol (NNTP)
- Exchange Message Transfer Agent (MTA) Stacks
- Exchange Post Office Protocol version 3 (POP3)
- Exchange Internet Message Access Protocol version 4 (IMAP4)
- Exchange Routing Engine

If you remove SharePoint Portal Server from an Exchange 2000 server, Exchange will continue to work.

11.15 Microsoft SQL Server and SharePoint Portal Server

If you install SharePoint Portal Server on a computer running Microsoft SQL Server 7.0 or SQL Server 2000, SharePoint Portal Server will upgrade the existing MSSearch. In addition, SharePoint Portal Server upgrades the full-text index format of all the existing indexes on that computer the next time MSSearch starts. For the upgrade to succeed there must be enough disk space on the computer to accommodate 120 percent of the size of the largest full-text index on the drive. Upgrading the full-text index format can take several hours, depending on the number and size of the existing indexes. During the SharePoint Portal Server setup, a message informs you that the service will be upgraded.

Because SharePoint Portal Server upgrades MSSearch and full-text indexes, do not install SharePoint Portal Server on a server that participates in a SQL Server clustering environment or add a computer running Share-Point Portal Server to a clustered environment.

You can install SQL Server on a computer already running SharePoint Portal Server. In this instance, SQL Server uses MSSearch installed by SharePoint Portal Server. If you remove SharePoint Portal Server from a computer that has SQL Server installed, SharePoint Portal Server will not remove the upgraded MSSearch, because it is a shared service with SQL Server.

Glossary

ADO (ActiveX Data Objects)

Object interface into the OLEDB programming interface.

ADO .NET

API in .NET for data access.

ACL

Access Control List. Contains lists of users and their appropriate permissions.

AIC

Application Integration Component. Software that allows BizTalk Server to send documents and files to a line of business applications.

ASCII

American Standard Code for Information Interchange. A computer character set and collating sequence.

ANSI

American National Standards Institute. A leading force behind the SQL standard.

Assembly

A collection of code and associated elements that comprises a Microsoft .NET solution created in Visual Studio .NET.

Authenticode

A framework that allows a developer to include digital signature information about programming code, including author details.

Batch File

A number of Transact-SQL statements executed together either interactively or from a file.

Blob

Binary Large Object. A datatype used for storing unstructured data such as pictures, sound or video. The actual datatype used in SQL Server is the image datatype.

BizTalk Initiative

Industrywide initiative designed to encourage the use of XML in business-to-business transactions. See www.biztalk.org.

Checkpoint

A mechanism that ensures that completed transactions are written from cache to the database at frequent intervals.

CLB

Component Load Balancing. Technique to spread a workload across components equally to improve processing throughput.

Clustered Index

A type of index where the physical order of the data in the table is the same as the order in the index. There can only be one clustered index per table.

Column

A relational model term that equates to a field. Also called an attribute.

COM+

The latest edition of COM with better support for transactions and the development of Internet-based applications.

Commit

A statement that finishes a transaction and makes all changes to the database permanent.

Composite Key

Any type of key that comprises of one of more columns.

Concurrency

The simultaneous use of a database by a number of users.

CSV

Comma Separated Value. A common format that data is placed into when exported from many computer systems. Uses commas to separate data values.

Data Definition Language

The statements that describe the metadata definitions.

Data Manipulation Language

The statements that allow data in a SQL Server database to be stored, retrieved, modified, or deleted.

Data Transformation Services (DTS)

A SQL Server data pump that allows data to be imported or exported from SQL Server while being scrubbed or massaged.

Database

A collection of data which usually more than one user can access at the same time. The database maintains its own data integrity and security. There can, and typically will be, be a number of databases per SQL Server.

DCOM

Distributed version of COM. Permits COM applications to communicate between different physical servers.

Distributed iNternet Architecture (DNA)

A multilayered approach to software design architecture created by Microsoft. By using a DNA approach, developers separate the user interface from the business logic and database store.

Distributed Transaction Coordinator (DTC)

A tool that manages transactions across multiple SQL Servers.

DNA

See Distributed iNternet Architecture.

DTD

Document Type Definition. Describes how tags and nesting levels may be used in an XML document.

EAI

Enterprise Application Integration. The process of linking different IT systems together, often with difficult-to-manage interfaces.

EDI

Electronic Data Interchange. Industrywide standard for sending inter-company business data.

EDIFACT

Electronic Data Interchange for Administration, Commerce, and Transport. An EDI standard.

EDI850

An EDI-based standard for data interchange.

Embedded SQL

SQL code that is embedded in an application and precompiled before execution.

GXA

Global XML Architecture. An IBM and Microsoft initiative to improve standards around Web Services.

Hash Value

The result of applying a cryptographic hash function to a piece of data.

HTTP

HyperText Transfer Protocol. An Internet standard protocol for connecting systems across the World Wide Web.

HTTPS

HyperText Transfer Protocol/Secure. A secure version of HTTP (qv).

HTML

HyperText Markup Language. A format used to publish documents on the World Wide Web.

IETF

Internet Engineering Task Force. Voluntary body that defines and manages open technical standards on the Internet.

IIS

Internet Information Server. Microsoft's Web server product.

Index

A structure within the database that locates a row based on a key value.

IL

Intermediary language used by .NET in the CLR.

ISAPI

Internet Server API. A programming interface used with Microsoft Internet Information Server.

ISO

International Standards Organization. Promotes the use of standards across many industries worldwide.

Kerberos

A network-based authentication protocol using secret key cryptography.

Microsoft Management Console (MMC)

The host for SQL Server Enterprise Manager and other back-office administration tools.

Microsoft Transaction Server (MTS)

Software that manages the middle-layer business objects in a DNA application.

NLB

Network Load Balancing. A technique that shares network traffic across multiple servers to improve processing throughput.

ODBC

Open Database Connectivity Microsoft's defacto standard for PC-client access to database servers.

OLAP

OnLine Analytical Processing. The multidimensional view of a data set. Often used in the context of data warehouse cubes.

OLAP Services

The component of SQL Server that enables data warehouse cubes to be built and managed. Known as PLATO during SQL Server 7.0 development and beta test.

OLEDB

The preferred data-access interface supported by Microsoft. Designed for accessing both relational and nonrelational data sources.

OLTP

Online Transaction Processing. An environment that supports many users performing the same critical business functions. Typically, an OLTP system is made up of many simultaneous users, all performing the same function, such as taking orders or seat reservations.

Relational Database

A database model that describes data as a set of independent tables. Within each table, the data is organized into rows and columns.

Resource

Content Management Server multimedia (e.g., graphics, videos) files that can be added to Web pages.

S/MIME

Secure Multipurpose Internet Mail Extension, which provides a standard way of encrypting browser-based e-mail.

Security

The protection of the data held in the database against unauthorized access.

SOAP

Simple Object Access Protocol. A Web-based standard that allows distributed applications to work across the Web using a combination of XML and HTTP.

SQL

Structured Query Language. The standard query language for accessing relational databases. It is an official standard comprised both a data-definition and a data-manipulation language.

SQL Distributed Management Objects (SQL-DMO)

A layer of management objects forming a hierarchy, with the primary SQL Server object containing databases, which in turn contain tables, views, and stored procedure objects. Used by the SQL Enterprise Manager and Visual Basic for Applications.

SQL Enterprise Manager

The graphical SQL Server management tool. Can be used to administer SQL Servers distributed around a network and to create and edit SQL Server objects, such as databases, tables, and login IDs.

SQL Executive

The component of SQL Server responsible for the management of administrative tasks, such as the alerting of operators.

SQL Name Space (SQL-NS)

A complimentary service to SQL DMO allowing access to Enterprise Manager functions.

tModel

Taxonomy model used to describe a service or organization within UDDI.

Transaction

The grouping of a number of Transact-SQL statements together such that all their changes are applied to the database or none of them are.

Transaction Log

A file that contains all the data structures modified during a transaction. The journal file is used to reconstruct the database and maintain integrity during a system or application failure.

Transaction Processing

A style of computing supporting multiple users performing predefined tasks against a shared database.

UDDI

Universal Description, Discovery, and Integration. A Web-based initiative to make services and products easier to find electronically across the World Wide Web.

URL

Uniform Resource Locator. Formal name for a Web site address on the World Wide Web.

W3C

World Wide Web Consortium. A group responsible for setting and maintaining technical standards across the World Wide Web.

WebDAV

Web Document Authoring and Versioning. A standard for the collaborative creation of documents across the World Wide Web.

Windows NT

One of Microsoft's 32-bit server operating systems.

X/Open

An independent, worldwide, open-systems organization that is supported by most of the leading information-system suppliers, software companies, and user organizations.

XML

eXtensible Markup Language. A self-describing data-transfer language used on the Internet.

XPATH

A language used by XSLT and XPointer to address parts of an XML document.

Guide to Microsoft .NET Products System Requirements

The Microsoft range of .NET products requires a minimum specification of hardware to run. This is a minimum and each specific installation will be different, so this is to be treated as a guide only. For up-to-date information about any latest service packs or hardware recommendations that may be required for a particular installation, visit the Microsoft Web site (www.microsoft.com).

Microsoft Windows 2000 Server (Minimum Requirements)

- Computer/Processor

  133 MHz or higher Pentium-compatible CPU

- Memory

  256MB of RAM recommended minimum. (128MB minimum supported; 4GB maximum)

- Hard Disk

  2GB hard-disk with a minimum of 1.0GB free space. (Additional free hard-disk space is required if you are installing over a network.)

- CPU Support

  Windows 2000 Server supports up to four CPUs on one machine.

Microsoft Application Center 2000 (Minimum Requirements)

- Processor

  Pentium-compatible 400 MHz or higher processor

- Operating System

  Microsoft Windows 2000 Server or Windows 2000 Advanced Server operating system, Microsoft Windows 2000 Service Pack 1 or later, and Microsoft Internet Information Services 5.0 must be installed as part of Windows 2000 installation.

- Memory

  256MB of RAM minimum recommended.

- Hard Disk

  100MB of available hard-disk space to install services; additional space required for site content and databases.

- Drive

  CD-ROM drive

- Display

  Windows 2000-compatible video graphics adapter with 800x600 minimum resolution.

- Mouse

  Microsoft Mouse or compatible pointing device.

- Other Devices

  One Network Interface Card (two recommended); if using Windows 2000 Network Load Balancing, two Network Integration Cards are required.

Cient Components (Minimum Requirements)

- Processor

  Pentium-compatible 266 MHz or higher processor

- Operating System

  Microsoft Windows 2000 Professional, Windows 2000 Server, or Windows 2000 Advanced Server operating system, with Microsoft Windows 2000 Service Pack 1 or later.

- Memory

  128MB of RAM minimum recommended

- Hard Disk

  20MB of available hard-disk space

- Drive

  CD-ROM drive

- Display

  Windows 2000–compatible video graphics adapter with 800×600 minimum resolution.

- Mouse

  Microsoft Mouse or compatible pointing device.

- Other Devices

  Network adapter card

Microsoft BizTalk Server 2002 (Minimum Requirements)

- Processor

  Computer with a Pentium 300 MHz or higher processor

- Operating System

  For production use:

  Microsoft Windows 2000 Server or Windows 2000 Advanced Server with Service Pack 2 (SP2) or later.

  For tools-only installations:

  Windows 2000 Server, Windows 2000 Advanced Server, Windows 2000 Professional with SP2 or later, or Windows XP Professional or later.

- Memory

  256MB of RAM

- Hard Disk

  6GB of available hard-disk space

- Drive

  CD-ROM drive

- Display

  VGA or higher-resolution monitor, Super VGA (SVGA) recommended

- Mouse

  Microsoft Mouse or compatible pointing device.

- Other Devices

  Network adapter card

Microsoft Commerce Server 2002 (Minimum Requirements)

- Processor

  Computer with a Pentium-compatible 400 MHz or higher processor

- Operating System

  Microsoft Windows 2000 Server or Windows 2000 Advanced Server with Service Pack 2 (SP2) or later and Security Release Package 1 (SRP1) or later

- Memory

  256MB of RAM

- Hard Disk

  100MB of available hard-disk space to install services. Additional space required for site content and databases.

  NTFS-formatted hard-disk volume

- Drive

  CD-ROM drive

- Display

  Windows 2000-compatible video graphics adapter with 800 x 600 minimum resolution

- Mouse

  Microsoft Mouse or compatible pointing device.

- Other Devices

  Network adapter card, Microsoft SQL Server 2000 with Analysis Services and SP2 or later

Microsoft Content Management Server 2002 (Minimum Requirements)

- Processor

  Intel Pentium or compatible 166 MHz or higher processor

- Operating System

  Microsoft Windows 2000 Server operating system

- Memory

  128MB of RAM, 256MB recommended

- Hard Disk

  500MB of free disk space on the hard-disk where you install Exchange 2000

- Drive

  CD-ROM drive

- Display

  VGA monitor

Microsoft Host Integration Server 2002 (Minimum Requirements)

- Processor

  Computer with a Pentium 90 MHz or higher processor

- Operating System

  Windows NT Server 4.0 with Service Pack 6a or later, Microsoft Windows 2000 Server, Windows 2000 Advanced Server, or Windows 2000 Datacenter Server operating system

- Memory

  128MB of RAM

- Hard Disk

  120MB available hard-disk space

- Drive

  CD-ROM drive

- Display

  VGA or higher-resolution monitor

Internet Security and Acceleration Server 2000 Enterprise Edition

- 300 MHz or higher Pentium II–compatible CPU
- Microsoft Windows 2000 Server or Windows 2000 Advanced Server with Service Pack 1 or later, or Windows 2000 Datacenter Server operating system
- 256MB of RAM
- 20MB of available hard-disk space

  One local hard-disk partition formatted with the NTFS

- Microsoft Windows 2000 compatible network adapter for communicating with the internal network

  Additional Windows 2000 compatible network adapter, modem, or ISDN adapter for communicating with the Internet or an upstream server

  To implement the array and advanced policies configuration, you also need Windows Active Directory on your network.

Microsoft Operations Manager (Minimum Requirements)

- Processor

  550 MHz or higher Pentium-compatible processor

- Operating System

  Microsoft Windows 2000 Server, Advanced Server, or Datacenter Server operating system with Service Pack 2 or later

- Memory

  512MB of RAM

- Hard Disk

  1GB of available hard-disk space

- CD-ROM Drive

  Available for installation purposes

- Monitor

  Super VGA (800 x 600) or higher resolution

- Pointing Device

  Microsoft Mouse or compatible pointing device

- Database

  Microsoft SQL Server 2000 Standard or Enterprise Edition or later (recommended); Microsoft Access 2000 or later

Microsoft Project Server 2002 (Minimum Requirements)

- Processor

  Computer with a Pentium III 500 MHz or higher processor

- Operating System

Microsoft Windows 2000 Server with Service Pack 1 (SP1) or later, or Windows 2000 Advanced Server with SP1 or later

- Memory

RAM requirements depend on number of services installed on the computer. Minimum RAM requirements for Microsoft Project Server 2002:

- 128MB of RAM (Required)

Customers installing SharePoint Team Services from Microsoft require an additional 128MB of RAM.

Customers installing Microsoft SQL Server 2000 require an additional 64MB of RAM.

Customers installing SQL Server 2000 Analysis Services require an additional 64MB of RAM.

RAM requirements depend on number of services installed on the computer. Minimum RAM recommendations for Microsoft Project Server 2002:

- 512MB of RAM (Recommended)

Customers installing SharePoint Team Services: additional 192MB of RAM recommended.

Customers installing SQL Server 2000: additional 128MB of RAM recommended.

Customers installing SQL Server 2000 Analysis Services: additional 128MB of RAM recommended.

- Hard Disk

Hard disk space requirements depend on number of services installed on the computer.

50MB of available hard-disk space is required for the typical installation of Microsoft Project Server 2002.

Customers installing SharePoint Team Services require an additional 70MB for a typical installation, plus 5MB for each provisioned Web site.

Customers installing SQL Server 2000 require an additional 250MB for the typical installation of SQL Server.

Customers installing SQL Server 2000 Analysis Services require an additional 130MB for the typical installation of Analysis Services.

Note: Installing additional services requires more hard-disk space.

Hard disk space requirements depend on number of services installed on the computer.

- Drive

  CD-ROM drive

- Display

  Super VGA (800 _ 600) or higher-resolution monitor with 256 colors

  Super VGA (800 _ 600) or higher-resolution monitor with 256 colors

- Mouse

  Microsoft Mouse, Microsoft IntelliMouse, or compatible pointing device

- Programs

  Listed below are the programs required for data storage and management:

  SQL Server 2000 or later or the included Microsoft SQL Server 2000 Desktop Engine (MSDE 2000) is required for server data storage needs.

  SQL Server 2000 or later is required for enterprise project and resource management.

  Microsoft Internet Information Services (IIS) version 5.0 or later.

Microsoft Mobile Information Server 2002 (Minimum Requirements)

- Processor

  Server with 500 MHz or higher Pentium II–compatible processor (dual processor recommended)

- Operating System

  Microsoft Windows 2000 Server with Service Pack 2 (SP2) or later, or Windows 2000 Advanced Server with SP2 (for clustering)

- Memory

  256MB of RAM (512MB recommended)

- Hard Disk

  50MB of available hard-disk space

- Drive

  CD-ROM or DVD-ROM drive

- Display

  VGA or higher resolution

- Mouse

  Microsoft Mouse, Microsoft IntelliMouse, or compatible pointing device

- Other Devices

  Microsoft Exchange Server 5.5 with SP4 or Exchange 2000 Server with SP2 installed on a separate server for use with Microsoft Outlook Mobile Access 2002 and notifications

  High-speed connection to the wireless network (private digital leased line or existing Internet connection)

Microsoft SQL Server 2000 (Minimum Requirements)

- Processor

  Intel Pentium or compatible 166 MHz or higher processor.

- Operating System

  SQL Server 2000 Enterprise Edition and Standard Edition run on Microsoft Windows 2000 Server, Windows 2000 Advanced Server, Windows 2000 Datacenter Server operating systems, Microsoft Windows NT Server version 4.0 Service Pack 5 (SP5) or later, and Windows NT Server 4.0 Enterprise Edition with SP5 or later

  SQL Server 2000 trial software and SQL Server 2000 Developer Edition run on the operating systems listed above for the Enterprise and Standard Editions, as well as on Windows XP Professional, Windows XP Home Edition, Windows 2000 Professional, and Windows NT Workstation 4.0 with SP5 or later.

  SQL Server 2000 Personal Edition and SQL Server 2000 Desktop Engine run on the operating systems listed above for Enterprise and Standard Editions, as well as on Windows 98, Windows Millennium Edition (Windows Me), Windows XP Professional, Windows XP Home Edition, Windows 2000 Professional, and Windows NT Workstation 4.0 with SP5 or later.

- Memory

Enterprise Edition: 64MB RAM; 128MB recommended.

Standard Edition: 64MB.

Evaluation Edition: 64MB; 128MB recommended.

Developer Edition: 64MB.

Personal Edition: 128MB for Windows XP; 64MB for Windows 2000; 32MB for other operating systems.

Desktop Engine: 128MB for Windows XP; 64MB for Windows 2000; 32MB for other operating systems.

- Hard Disk

Enterprise, Standard, Evaluation, Developer, and Personal Editions require:

95–270MB free hard-disk space for the server; 250MB for a typical installation.

50MB free hard-disk space for a minimum installation of Analysis Services; 130MB for a typical installation.

80MB free hard-disk space for English Query (supported on the Windows 2000 operating system but not logo certified).

Desktop Engine requires 44MB of available hard-disk space.

- Drive

CD-ROM drive

- Display

VGA or higher-resolution monitor

- Other Devices

Microsoft Internet Explorer version 5.0 or later.

Windows 95, Windows 98, Windows Me, Windows NT 4.0, Windows 2000 and Windows XP have built-in network software. Additional network software is required if you are using Banyan VINES or AppleTalk ADSP. Novell NetWare IPX/SPX client support is provided by the NWLink protocol of Windows-based networking.

- Client Support

Windows 954, Windows 98, Windows Me, Windows NT Workstation 4.0, Windows 2000 Professional, Windows XP Professional, and Windows XP Home Edition are supported.

UNIX, Apple Macintosh, and OS/2 require Open Database Connectivity (ODBC) client software from a third-party vendor.

Microsoft Visual Studio .NET (Minimum Requirements)

- Processor

  Personal computer (PC) with a Pentium II–class processor, 450 megahertz (MHz)

- Operating System

  Microsoft Windows XP Professional

  Microsoft Windows 2000 Professional

  Microsoft Windows 2000 Server

  Microsoft Windows NT 4.0 Workstation

  Microsoft Windows NT 4.0 Server

  (Note: Microsoft Windows Millennium Edition and Windows NT 4.0 Terminal Server are not supported.)

- Memory

  Microsoft Windows XP Professional:

  160MB of RAM

  Windows 2000 Professional:

  96MB of RAM

  Windows 2000 Server:

  192MB of RAM

  Windows NT 4.0 Workstation:

  64MB of RAM

  Windows NT 4.0 Server:

  160MB of RAM

- Hard Disk:

  Standard Edition:

  2.5GB on installation drive, which includes 500MB on system drive

  Professional and Enterprise Editions

  3.5 GB on installation drive, which includes 500MB on system drive

- Drive

  CD-ROM or DVD-ROM drive

- Display

  Super VGA (800 x 600) or higher-resolution monitor with 256 colors

- Mouse

  Microsoft Mouse or compatible pointing device

Microsoft .NET Framework (Minimum Requirements)

- Processor

  Intel Pentium class, 90 MHz or higher

- Operating System

  Microsoft Windows 2000, with the latest Windows service pack and critical updates available from the Microsoft security Web site.

  Microsoft Windows XP

  Microsoft Windows NT 4.0

  Windows Millennium Edition (Windows ME)

  Windows 98

  Minimum RAM Requirements

  32MB (96MB or higher recommended)

- Hard Disk

  Hard disk space required to install: 160MB

  Hard disk space required: 70MB

- Display

  Video: 800 x 600, 256 colors

- Input Device

  Microsoft Mouse or compatible pointing device

- Other

  Microsoft Internet Explorer 5.01 or later is required.

  Microsoft Data Access Components 2.6 are required.

Index